D0723585

THE
PENNY PINCHER'S
WINE GUIDE

Avon Books are available at special quantity discounts for bulk purchases for sales promotions, premiums, fund raising or educational use. Special books, or book excerpts, can also be created to fit specific needs.

For details write or telephone the office of the Director of Special Markets, Avon Books, Dept. FP, 1790 Broadway, New York, New York 10019, 212-399-1357.

THE
PENNY PINCHER'S
WINE GUIDE

LUCY WAVERMAN

Text illustrations by Jude Waples

AVON BOOKS OF CANADA
PUBLISHERS OF BARD, CAMELOT, DISCUS AND FLARE BOOKS

To Bruce, without whose help and care
this book would never have been finished.

THE PENNY PINCHER'S WINE GUIDE is an original
publication of Avon Books. This work has never before
appeared in book form.

AVON BOOKS OF CANADA
A division of
The Hearst Corporation
2061 McCowan Road
Scarborough, Ontario M1S 3Y6
Canada

Copyright © 1983 by Lucy Waverman
Text illustrations Copyright © 1983 by Jude Waples
Published by arrangement with the author
Library of Congress Catalog Card Number: 83-91110
ISBN: 0-380-85027-3

All rights reserved, which includes the right to
reproduce this book or portions thereof in any form
whatsoever except as provided by the U.S. Copyright Law.
For information address Avon Books of Canada.

First Avon Printing, November, 1983

AVON TRADEMARK REG. U.S. PAT. OFF. AND IN
OTHER COUNTRIES, MARCA REGISTRADA, HECHO EN
U.S.A.

Printed in Canada

WEB 10 9 8 7 6 5 4 3 2 1

ACKNOWLEDGMENTS

It's impossible to write this kind of book in isolation. Without the help and support of many others it would be just another good idea.

My expert tasting panel gave their time, palates and patience to evaluate the wines. Thank you to Tom Bjarnson, David Stockwood, Dinah Koo, Allison Cumming, Gerard Chouest, Tisa Starr, Robert Black, Margaret Swaine, Betty Van der Ree, Gary Galt, Brian Lippiatt, and Tom Hitchman. In particular, a special thank you to Frank Baldock, who turned words into living images to describe the wines, and Gail Donner, my partner in the previous edition, who took time from her very busy schedule to write reams of notes and information.

The expert tasters from the provinces other than Ontario tracked down wines, arranged tastings, took copious notes and then molded the words into the succinct phrases which are used in the book. J. J. and Anne Camp from British Columbia, Cynthia Milsom and Don MacLean from Alberta, Jack and Margo Toole from Manitoba and Alan Mills from Quebec, did a marvelous job.

The Canadian wine companies not only contributed wines but also gave me lots of background information. Thanks to Andres Wines Ltd., Barnes Wines Ltd., Brights Wines Ltd., Château des Charmes Wines Ltd., Château Gai Wines Ltd., Inniskillin Wines Inc., and Jordan Wines.

Many of the wine importers across Canada trusted us enough to give us tasting samples. Special thanks to Denny Dunlop at William Mara Co. who was the first to encourage us. He was quickly followed by Alberta Distillers and Carrington Imports Ltd., Hudson's Bay Distillers Ltd., Basil D. Hobbs Inc., Cana Import Wine Agency, Cipelli Wines and Spirits Inc., Cosmopolitan Wine Agents Ltd., Distillers Co. (Canada) Ltd., Emu Australian Wines Ltd., English Gunn Ltd., FBM Distillery, Fred M. Gaby and Co., Galilee Wines, Hoch Wines, Hiram Walker and Sons Ltd.,

International Vintners Ltd., Jack Baker Distillers Ltd., Les Lyons Imports Inc., McGuinness Distillers Ltd., Mark Anthony Wine Merchants Inc., Meagher's Distillery Ltd., Melchers Inc., Martin Lacey, Pelwin Agencies and Watleys, Peter Mielzynski Agencies, Rieder Distillery Ltd., Schenley-Park and Tilford Wine and Spirits Agency, Sainsbury Ltd., Schiralli Saverio Agencies Ltd., Superior Wine Ltd., and Vintage Wines and Spirits Ltd.

I'm deeply indebted to all the people who attended the tastings—they were the backbone of the book—and The Cooking School students who tasted as they cooked!

Leona Chase from The Cheese Wheel in Toronto was most generous in sharing her cheese expertise, and Karen Bolton helped the tastings run smoothly.

Special thanks to Zoe Cormack Jones who organized everything, especially me, and generally kept everything on track.

To my husband Bruce MacDougall, who programmed the computer, listed the wines, put his imprint on the tastings, and encouraged me when I was down, heartfelt gratitude.

And thanks to Emma, Katie, and Sandy, our children, who learned how to wrap bottles in foil, open and pour wine, and even to taste it; their support was heartwarming.

CONTENTS

INTRODUCTION

Alexis Lichine, the great wine writer and winemaker, when asked about the liquor control boards in Canada, visibly shuddered. Joe Heitz, that excellent Californian winemaker, said he wouldn't even try to have his wines listed in Canada because the paper work alone took too much time.

Liquor control is not a blessing. The system gives us quality control and standard wine lists across the country, but we miss out on charming wines from tiny vineyards because producers couldn't sell or even supply their quotas. Fine wines are barely accessible to people who do not live in major cities where there are specialty wine stores. They are hardly affordable, at any rate. There are no loss leader sales or even just ordinary bargains unless the label has fallen off or the wine is about to be delisted. We are controlled by our liquor boards which, in turn are controlled by the provincial governments. Taxes and federal and provincial markups account for well over 50 percent of the retail price.

So we have standard wine lists. We also have a dizzying array of wines from which to choose. When I enter a liquor store I am amazed at the selection and how little I know about many of the labels.

Although sometimes there are wine consultants available to help us choose, I feel that as consumers we deserve to have more information at our fingertips.

Hence the book. I have listed, described, and commented on the wines under $8.00 available through our provincial liquor boards. I have tried to cover as many as possible, but due to unavailability, oversight, or time limitations, more wines than I would like have been missed.

This is a consumer's guide. Consumers have tasted the wines alongside experts, and it is from their viewpoint that this book has been written.

In some instances there have been wide differences in opinion between consumer and professional. We have walked a middle line in those cases. Most wines have drawn similar responses from both groups.

Food complements wine. As much of my expertise lies in the food area, I have included menus and recipes for both party and family meals. I have also suggested suitable wines to drink with them.

I hope this book will be a useful guide when you are faced with unfamiliar wine bottles, confusing wine situations, or when you are simply searching for more information about the world's favorite libation.

Cheers.

PART ONE
THE
WINES

Fill every beaker up, my men,
pour forth the cheering wine:
There's life and strength in every drop,
thanksgiving to the vine!

—ALBERT GREEN

WINES OF THE WORLD

CANADA

In an earlier edition of Penny Pincher's I reported optimistically that "there was hope . . . for the domestic product."

Recent tastings in Europe and at home are beginning to show my optimism was justified. Further confirmation is found in the sales figures which have increased dramatically since the mid 70's, particularly in British Columbia and Ontario.

Most of the better Canadian table wines are now being made of hybrid grapes which are the result of many years of experimental crossbreeding between European vines and hardy native varieties. Examples include Seyval Blanc, a medium dry, slightly spicy white and Maréchal Foch, a dry, medium bodied, very fruity red. These inexpensive wines made from a variety of grapes are also the backbone of the Canadian blends. These blends are cutting heavily into the sales of imported wines.

One step up from the hybrids and still climbing are the home grown versions of the great European varietals. The Riesling of Germany has taken root not only on the hills of the Okanagan Valley, which shares the same latitude as Germany, but is also grown in Ontario's Niagara Peninsula. Distinctive and tasty wines also are being made from Burgundy's Chardonnay grape and the Gamay of Beaujolais.

The remainder of the wine sold in Canadian labeled bottles is made either from the native grape varieties or from imported juice. The purely domestic product is very fruity with a strong, characteristically "foxy" smell and taste.

In Quebec, Canadian-made wines from primarily foreign grapes receive preferential tax treatment. They are not particularly impressive, but they are inexpensive.

In summary, there are now many excellent Canadian wines being made and some remarkable values to be had in the range of wines available.

Nevertheless, on average, the homegrown product continues to lag behind its foreign competition. Continued improvement will close the gap, and I feel justified in my hope that in a few short years the tables will be turned. When this happens much of the credit must go to the dedicated winemaking pioneers across the country.

BRITISH COLUMBIA

In British Columbia the provincial government supported the creation of an estate wine industry in the Okanagan Valley over which it exercises rigid control. It restricts each winery to two liquor board listings, puts a limit on the quantity of wine each grower can produce, and insists on the use of British Columbian grapes.

Bob and Lee Claremont of Claremont Estate Winery and Vineyards find the system frustrating, but love the challenge and the way of life. The Claremonts are experimenting in an effort to find a distinctive Okanagan Valley style for their wines.

Bob, formerly chief winemaker of a much larger establishment, suggests that Claremont's Okanagan

Riesling, a medium dry, fruity wine with a very distinctive, almost earthy flavor, is representative of the several available at the winery and of his developing Okanagan style.

Sumac Ridge was, and is, an Okanagan Valley golf club, but now it is also a winery where Harry McWatters and Lloyd Schmidt make and sell their wine.

Harry and Lloyd are seeking the quintessential dry Okanagan white and think they may have found it in their Sumac Ridge Chenin Blanc, bone dry but fruity, subtle and soft.

The Grey Monk Cellars of Trudy and George Heiss overlook Lake Okanagan, but the Heisses are looking to the Rhine for inspiration. Just a mouthful of their Grey Monk Pinot Auxerrois, a crisp, light, and delicate wine in the German style, reveals the clarity of that vision.

The Auxerrois, a Johannisberg Riesling, and a Gewurztraminer are included in the several wines in the German style available from Grey Monk.

At Kelowna's Uniacke the Mitchells, from Nova Scotia, offer a Merlot (the great wine of St. Emilion) in a lighter, fresher style, and a Pinot Noir. But as with the others in the valley, Uniacke's best wines at this early stage of development (and, I predict, for a long time to come) are made from the traditional great grapes of Germany, including the Rhine or Johannisberg Riesling, and the Gewurztraminer.

ONTARIO

The Ontario government, although supportive of its smaller wineries in other ways, has not adopted the British Columbian estate winery structure. With hard work, considerable talent and the luck of the sun, the industry has done well without that structure and continues to make great forward strides.

With flair in the marketplace and skill in the winery, Niagara's Inniskillin has led the way for Ontario's producers. Deep in color, full-bodied but round and smooth, Inniskillin's 1980 Maréchal Foch is believed by many to be the best red wine yet produced in this country. And as a result of the able and extensive marketing of Don Ziraldo and Karl Kaiser, it can be purchased in France and the United States along with others in the Inniskillin stable.

Not far from Inniskillin Paul Bosc, of Château des Charmes who learned his trade in Burgundy, is using Burgundian Chardonnay grapes to make wine whose quality is giving the original real competition. And when price is considered it makes the Château des Charmes 1981 Estate Chardonnay, with a rich, buttery flavor and plenty of fruit, a bargain indeed. Several other wines of good to excellent quality are produced by Château des Charmes, including Canada's first commercial Cabernet Sauvignon.

In southwestern Ontario, a microclimate favors the husband and wife team of Charlotte and Allan Eastman of Charal winery. Their Chardonnays have won prizes, but for the Eastmans prizes are for show. Their real goal is the making of good wine at a reasonable price, and this goal is being achieved. Charal's Seyval Blanc is full of fruit with a soft, delicate, complex flavor, and at the price it is hard to beat.

Colio, near Windsor, is the new boy on the Ontario street, and to date its regular blends have been unexceptional. At the upper end of its range, however, the story is different. One of Colio's premium wines, Riserva Rosso, a hearty red wine with lots of flavor, has real potential.

We have now touched on most of the significant small Canadian wineries. Of course, there are more and some of these are growing in size and reputation as the quality of their product improves. Podamer, the Ontario's "champagne" producer now has commendable table wines on the Ontario market as does Newark, a tiny operation at Niagara on the Lake. In Alberta Andrew Wolf, the creator of Baby Duck, is making wine in the foothills of the Rockies. In the Annapolis Valley of Nova Scotia another small winery is thriving. Some wine is even being made from Quebec-grown grapes.

Many dedicated professionals from the country's major wineries must also share in the accolades for the improvement of the homegrown product. This is particularly true in the lower price range where excellent blends such as Brights Entre Lac, Jordan Toscano, Andres Hochtaller, Château Gai Sparkling Alpenweiss, and Barnes Heritage Claret can be found.

Thus, while Canadian wines have room to grow to match the great European varieties, the efforts of large and small wineries in producing such straightforward, sound wines at reasonable prices can be enjoyed by all wine lovers.

CHILE

Chile makes the best wines in South America. Good soil and climate have helped, as has strict government control over the industry.

Growers cannot exceed their production quotas, which encourages them to grow good grapes. Wines must also reach certain standards before they can be exported. Both reds and whites are produced. The wines are named after the grape variety with which they are made, such as Cabernet-Sauvignon and Riesling.

FRANCE

As well as telling you the area in which the wine was produced, the label on a French wine bottle can give you a lot of other information if you know how to read it. Here are some wine label terms:

Château The estate where the grapes are grown.

Mis en bouteilles au château Bottled at the château. This means the wine will be shipped in the bottle, not in a cask. Châteaus usually bottle their best wine and ship the rest to a négociant.

Négociant The shipper who buys the wine, ages it, and then bottles or blends it with other wines. It is important to use reliable shippers.

Supérieur   The wine has 1% more alcohol than usual for
its type.

Appellation Contrôlée (AC)   The guarantee that the
growers have adhered to the highest standards set by
the government body regulating the French wine industry. AC laws regulate the number of vines planted
per acre, how they are pruned, how the wine is made,
and which areas may use the region name. This
prevents an area name (e.g., Bordeaux or Burgundy)
from being used for poor quality wines produced in
those regions.

Vin Délimités de Qualité Supérieure (VDQS)   Another
quality control, the standards of which are less strin-
gent. The quality of the wines with this designation is
generally not quite as high as those with the *appellation
contrôlée* designation but can still be very good.

Vin de Pays   The lowest ranked wines that are still quality
controlled.

BORDEAUX

Bordeaux wine sets the standard for winemakers around the
world. Many famous wines come from this region. In 1855
the red wines were classified into five "growths" established
on the basis of the average prices at that time. The most
expensive wines were classified as "first growth," and examples of these are Château Lafite and Château Lâtour. A
famous "second growth" wine is Ducru-Beaucaillou; a
well-known "third growth" wine is Château Palmer; a
"fourth growth" is Château Beychevelle; and a "fifth
growth" wine is Château Lynch Bages.

After the classified growths come the "bourgeois
growths," the middle class wines of the world. A "bourgeois
growth" wine such as Phélan Segur is excellent value, and
some of the wines in this classification can be successfully
laid down for a few years.

Sauterne is also one of the great white wine areas in the
Bordeaux region. The French Sauternes are made from
grapes which are picked when they are overripe and covered

in "noble rot," a kind of mold that dries out and sweetens the grape. The resulting wines are rich and sweet and expensive.

BURGUNDY

This large area produces a wide variety of wines, from the red Beaujolais which are best drunk young, to the white Burgundies and red wines of the Côte d'Or, which are among the world's greatest wines and improve with aging.

The wine-producing areas in Burgundy include Beaujolais, Maconnais, Chalonnais, Côte d'Or, Côte de Beaune, Côte de Nuits and Chablis. If a wine is labeled simply "Bourgogne," it is likely a blend. The great majority of Burgundy wines are blended by a shipper, and for that reason a Burgundy should be bought from a reliable shipper.

In recent years the fine wines of Burgundy have become extremely expensive.

ALSACE

Alsatian wines are white, fresh, crisp and spicy. Unlike the other French wines, they are named for the grape, not the area.

CORSICA

Corsica is a major producer of wines for blending. Its most notable wines are strong rosés, but it also produces some robust reds and whites.

LANGUEDOC

A very productive area for red wines, but with a few exceptions it produces only *vins ordinaires*.

LOIRE

This area in France covers over 600 square miles and produces light, fruity, charming wines of considerable variation—dry and sweet, still and sparkling, rosé, red, and white. The best are the whites, both sweet and dry.

PROVENCE

From Provence, lying on the Mediterranean, come orange-tinted rosés, strong and appealing. This area also produces some good whites and acceptable reds.

RHINE

The vineyards in this region are among the oldest in Europe, yet there is still good, virgin, wine-growing soil. The area is best known for the red wines which are warm and hearty like those of their Burgundy neighbor.

ROUSSILLON

This area produces large quantities of light red table wine and smaller quantities of white and rosé. Some of the sweeter wines are excellent.

GERMANY

The white wines of Germany are justifiably famous. The three main growing areas are the Rhine, the Palatinate and the Moselle. Many of the vineyards are planted along the slopes of the Rhine and Moselle Rivers. The two major grape varieties grown for German wines are the Sylvaner and the Riesling. The Sylvaner is used for the cheaper wines and the Riesling for the better quality product.

Rhine wines range from the complex and noble Rheingaus to the lighter, fresh table wines. The Palatinate wines are fine, mellow, smooth wines, sometimes very rich and sweet, similar to a French Sauterne. Moselle wines are light, fresh, and elegant, with a flowery bouquet. They are suitable for drinking throughout a meal or with dessert.

"Liebfraumilch" is probably the best known German wine term. It refers to a pleasant, easy-drinking wine which can come from any district but which maintains a traditional level of quality. It must be medium dry to medium soft, well balanced, and able to last three to four years in a bottle. A good shipper is the best guide to a good

Liebfraumilch. Today shippers tend to make distinctive bottles and labels so that the public will recognize their own particular brand.

German wine law is extremely complicated. The following classifications are for superior wines that need no sugar added to make them rich and well balanced. Each classification also implies a special degree of selection of the grapes.

Kabinett   Lowest ranking of the wines with no sugar added.

Spätlese   Made with late-picked grapes.

Auslese   Made with selected late-picked grapes, ranks higher than Spätlese.

Beerenauslese   Made with berries individually selected from bunches.

Trockenbeerenauslese   Made with selected overripe grapes covered with the noble rot, the highest ranking.

Trockenbeerenauslese wines are a superb ending to a fine dinner and are often drunk alone.

Good wine is also made from grapes that have had sugar added; it is labeled Qualitätswein. The lowest ranked controlled wine is the unpretentious Tafelwein.

GREECE

Retsina or resinated wine dates back to ancient Greece. It is a generic term for any wine flavored with pine resin. Retsina does not age well, is generally white, and is not terribly popular in North America.

Greece is now making ordinary reds and whites of no particular distinction.

HUNGARY

Characteristic Hungarian wine is white and sweet but full of fire. About 70% of the wine produced is white. The red exports are very popular with North Americans because they are of good quality and inexpensive. All wine is exported by the state wine agency. The most famous Hungarian wine is Egri Bikaver or Bull's Blood.

ISRAEL

Israel's climate makes it a promising wine producing country. Baron de Rothschild introduced French wine making methods there in 1882. He handed over the vineyards to the growers in 1906, and the industry has flourished since.

Originally noted for sweet, full-bodied, red wines of the dessert type, Israel is now producing dry reds and whites. Both their Cabernet Sauvignons and Sauvignon Blancs rank with wines of other countries.

ITALY

Italy is the largest wine producer in the world. It produces vast quantities of unpretentious blended wines which are decently made and of good value as well as great wines such as Barolo and Brunello di Montepulciano which are priced much more reasonably than the great French ones. Wines vary greatly from region to region as does the food, from rough and strong to light and delicate.

The vine grows readily in Italy, but it is only since 1963 that the government has introduced a quality control system. Under considerable pressure from France, whose market was being flooded with cheap Italian wines, control laws were set up in Italy. These are:

Simple denomination (Denominazione di Origine) Denotes wine with no official guarantee of quality, ordinary wines made from the traditional grape of an area.

Controlled denomination (Denominazione di Origine Controllata—DOC) Refers to wines reaching a stipulated standard of quality, but does not necessarily indicate a good wine. Even though the rules are adhered to, the individual talents of the winemaker affect the final product. These vineyards appear in an official register.

Controlled and guaranteed denomination (Denominazione di Origine Controllata e Garatita) Reserved for fine wines recommended by the Ministry of Agriculture and Forestry for quality and price. These winemakers must adhere to a very strict set of rules.

Vino da Tavola Is the category for all non DOC wines. Some great wines carry this label because they are outside DOC zones.

Despite a history of wine production which brings to mind images of rough, cheap, questionable wines in straw-covered bottles, the quality of Italian wines in recent years has risen considerably. Both fine and blended wines are now available all over the world. Canada imports more Italian wine than any other.

PORTUGAL

Portugal's climate is ideal for grape growing. The wines are pleasant, solid, and well made.

One of the most widely sold wines in the world is the famous Mateus Rosé which comes from the Vinhos Verdes area. Vinhos Verdes means green wine. These wines have a fresh, slightly fizzy taste and are inexpensive. The Dao wines come from north central Portugal where much more red than white wine is produced.

Port and Madeira are the finest wines that Portugal produces.

RUMANIA

Since World War II a planting program has increased the national vineyards in this country whose climate is very favorable to wine growing. Rumanian wines are becoming increasingly popular because both reds and whites, although not exciting, are straightforward and of good value.

SOUTH AFRICA

Traditionally South Africans were liquor drinkers, but now wines are gaining in popularity. Wine farmers in the past experienced many difficulties with overproduction, but now the constitutional body known as KWV controls prices and absorbs the surplus.

The once typical harsh, rough wines have given way to well made, light and full-bodied wines. Canada is a large market for South African wines, although in one province politics have driven them under the counter.

SPAIN

Spain is the third largest producer of wine in the world, but much of it is for home consumption. Because of climatic conditions wines range from the *vin ordinaire* of the central region to the full-bodied, tasty Riojas of Northern Spain. Climatic conditions also cause vintages to vary considerably from year to year. Look at the year as well as the shipper before you buy a Spanish wine. Torres, for example, is an excellent shipper.

Sherry is Spain's finest and most widely exported wine.

SWITZERLAND

The majority of Swiss wine is white. However, in recent years the Swiss have planted more red grapes. Gradually Swiss wines are being sold outside of Switzerland. At this time no Swiss wines are available in Canada.

The vineyards are efficient but do not produce great wines.

UNITED STATES

The majority of the wine produced in the United States comes from California, but wine is also produced in the Pacific Northwest, the Midwest, and the East, in particular, New York State.

CALIFORNIA

Wine production in California has increased 150% since 1970. The soil and climate are similar to those of other great wine producing countries, and excellent wine is being made. For many years mediocre grape varieties were planted which made indifferent wines at best, but huge amounts of money were spent on research, development and technology. California wine producers have made great strides in understanding climate and soil, so that the right grapes are grown under the right conditions. In 1970 Baron de Rothschild was quoted as saying that California wines were like "Coke." But he has been so impressed with the recent changes that he has gone into partnership with Robert Mondavi to produce premium California wines.

The most famous wine growing region in California is the Napa Valley. Napa grows Cabernet Sauvignon grapes (the primary grape of Bordeaux); and Chardonnay grapes, both of which make fine wines as well as good blended table wines. Small and large wineries are nestled together in the valley. Some of the larger ones export to Canada, but the wines from many of the smaller ones are sold directly from the winery so that some of the best California wine never leaves the state.

The Sonoma Valley runs parallel to Napa but is divided from it by the Mayacamas Mountains. Sonoma produces excellent table wines, good German-style whites, and good sparkling ones.

Wines in California are named for the grape variety from which they are made, for example, Chenin Blanc or Cabernet Sauvignon. Blends are given generic names such as Burgundy or Chablis. Zinfandel is the native grape of California and is used to make a delicious, fresh-berry tasting, red wine.

NEW YORK STATE

New York State wines are similar in nature to many Ontario wines. The native grape is the *labrusca* which gives the characteristic "foxy" taste associated with the wines of the area. It is losing in popularity to the hybrids which are crosses between *vinifera* grapes and native American varieties. Seyval Blanc and Maréchal Foch are examples of hybrid varieties which produce decent wines.

YUGOSLAVIA

Yugoslavia has a long winemaking history. It produces inexpensive, well made wine which ranges from light, fruity whites from the North to heavy, tannic reds from the South. Navip is the big Serbian cooperative which exports a great deal of its wine to Canada.

GLOSSARY OF WINE TERMS

As with all disciplines, the study of wine has a language all its own. Without this vocabulary, it is difficult to communicate your impressions of a wine. With it, you will dazzle your friends and relatives, waiters, and wine connoisseurs.

Acidity   The acid component which gives wine its freshness and crispness. Too little makes a flat, dull wine but too much can make an overly zesty or vinegary wine.

Aftertaste   The taste that comes back to the palate after the wine is swallowed.

Aroma   The smell of the grape.

Astringency   The tartness in the wine. The little nip it has.

Balance   The relationship between the different attributes of the wine. No characteristic (eg., acidity, sweetness, fruitiness) is overly pronounced; everything is in proportion.

Body   As with people, wine can be full and robust or light and thin. Do not be misled; a good wine can be light or fullbodied or in between.

Bouquet or nose   The smell of the wine. What the wine does to your nose.

Breathe   Can do wonders for red wine. Uncork the wine about an hour before, pour it into a decanter, and let it breathe—instant aging.

Clean   The unadulterated taste of the wine. No trace of the yeast or additives used in winemaking.

Complex   The combination of many different scents and flavors in the wine.

Dry   No trace of sweetness in the wine.

Finish   The final impression the wine makes as it goes down.

Flat   No oomph in the wine. A negative attribute.

Foxy   A characteristic pungency found in native Canadian grapes which strongly flavors the wine.

Fruity   The taste of the grape, not of the wine as a whole. Some wines are fruitier than others because of the type of grape used—a Riesling, for example.

Hybrids   A group of grape varieties produced by crossing some types of European grapes with native North American varieties.

Lay down   The storing of the wine. This allows it to age and improve in quality. Not all wines improve with aging, and some are best drunk young.

Legs   The church window effect that you get when wine is swirled around a glass and drips down the side. The better the legs, the more glycerine there is in the wine. Legs show potential in a wine.

Length   The time the flavor should remain with you. When the taste fades quickly and you feel you missed something, the wine is short.

Oak   The character the wine gets from the oak barrel that it ages in. There is much dissention as to what kind of oak should be used, although Limousin oak from France is considered the finest.

Sweet   The opposite of dry. Sweet wines contain a relatively large amount of unconverted grape sugar.

Tannin   An ingredient in the skin, pips, and stalk of the grapes which is very important in the aging process. In a young wine tannin gives a bitter, hard taste which dries the roof of the mouth.

Thin   Doesn't have roundness in the mouth. Lacks body.

Varietals   Used to describe the varieties of wines made from other than Canadian *labrusca*-type grapes.

Vin ordinaire   An undistinguished, everyday table wine.

Vintage   The year the wine was produced. Some years are better than others due to weather conditions.

Vitis labrusca   The Concord grape commonly grown in Canada for wine making purposes. See foxy.

Vitis vinifera   European varieties of grapes grown for wine making purposes.

Yeasty   The smell of the yeast in the bouquet. It is an undesirable quality except in newly bottled wines.

WINE
REVIEWS

*A naive little Burgundy,
but I think you'll be amused
by its presumption.*

—JAMES THURBER

The tasting summaries which follow are composites of the comments of many people.

Before starting I sought out a group of experts—mostly non-professional—and at each tasting the wines were tasted blind by several of the experts as well as a larger number of consumers. Tasters' opinions of the wines often differed, of course, but the best buy list represents the consensus achieved.

The composite notes for all wines tasted are included. Many that are not on the best buy list are sound wines of good quality. For my list I picked those wines which I felt rated highest, taking into consideration both price and quality.

After tasting over 600 wines available across the country and working with listings from all ten provinces as well as traveling across Canada to set up tastings and meet some of the Canadian producers, I feel I can make some comment on the approaches to wine taken by our provincial liquor boards. The treatment of wine varies enormously from province to province.

Alberta has the cheapest wines and the largest selection in its general listings. Its German list, particularly, is extensive and reasonably priced.

For French wines Quebec wins, hands down.

Variety, at least in wine, is not the spice of life on Prince Edward Island or in Nova Scotia, and the price levels in all the maritime provinces reflect the recognition by politicians of the value of wine to the provincial coffers.

The proximity of British Columbia to California is apparent in its list, but Saskatchewan, on the other side of the world from France, is the place to go for real French champagne.

In Manitoba you can obtain a bottle of luscious German Trockenbeerenauslese from the 1969 vintage (at considerable expense, mind you) whereas in New Brunswick the most expensive item is a 16-liter flask of a Canadian *vin ordinaire.*

In addition to their general lists each province has a specialty wine list, and items from that list can be ordered from any store.

British Columbia and Ontario, and to a lesser extent Alberta and Nova Scotia, have their own developing fine wine industries, and many special wine listings are available to residents of those provinces.

The following criteria were used to evaluate the wines. Everyone who participated in our wine tastings received a copy of these guidelines to use when scoring the wines. Perhaps when you are tasting you might like to follow these simple guidelines.

THE GUIDE

In tasting these wines, your immediate response is what we want. We would like you to jot down your brutally frank, gut reaction under the headings "Relative Sweetness," "Bouquet," and "Suitable With," as well as your general assessment under taste comments.

With this done, we would also like you to score the wine out of 20, keeping in mind that the wines are being compared to other inexpensive wines, and not to Château Lafite.

		Maximum Score
Appearance	Look for clarity and depth of color.	2
Bouquet	Any off-aroma, e.g., yeasty, acidic, should pull down the score. A positive bouquet, e.g., fruity, flowery, should do the opposite. Points off as well for no smell.	4
Taste	A good wine should have a fruity taste with some bite and body or power. It should not be too harsh, and the flavor should stay with you. Marks off for harshness, flatness, or no taste; sweetness that clings in your mouth; or taste you don't like.	10
Overall Quality	After you look at it, smell it and taste it. What is your general impression? Consider it in relation to other wines.	4
Total		20

PENNYPINCHER'S TASTING SUMMARY

WHITE WINES

REF. NO.	DESCRIPTION	PROVINCES AVAILABLE	RELATIVE SWEETNESS

AMERICAN

REF. NO.	DESCRIPTION	PROVINCES AVAILABLE	RELATIVE SWEETNESS
071258	Almaden Gewurz-traminer	O	sweet
066118	Almaden Johannis-berg Riesling	A	dryish
083782	Almaden Mountain Chablis	A S M O	off dry
063677	Almaden San Benito Chardonnay	A	off dry
079335	Andres Chablis	NS O	dryish
079343	Andres Chenin Blanc	BC O	somewhat dry
079350	Andres Johannisberg Riesling	BC	very sweet
079327	Andres Rhine	O	dryish
075671	Beringer Los Hermanos Chablis	A S O	dryish
030619	Christian Brothers Crystal Dry	M O NFLD	dry
023911	Colony Rhineskeller	BC A S	medium sweet
027565	Cribari Pinot Chardonnay	BC A O	dry
020487	Gallo California Pink Chablis	A PEI NFLD	burnt
004325	Gallo Chablis Blanc	BC A S M O Q NB NS PEI NFLD	hint of sweetness
067413	Gallo Rhine	A S M O NB NS PEI NFLD	semisweet

BOUQUET	TASTE COMMENTS	SUITABLE WITH
flowery, per-fumy	a heavy wine; taste resembles lichee nuts	Chinese desserts
earthy	hits the back of the mouth with a musty taste; forgettable	hospital food
not distin-guished	thinnish taste; initial bite but becomes quiet on the palate	food that's not fussy
nearly none	tart, some depth of flavor but harsh afterburn	ripe olives
strong raisin smell	soft and pleasant; very tasty; quaffable	asparagus
fruity, agreeable	light and very fruity, almost peachy; gets better as it goes along	friendly lunches
musty flowers	sweetness hides the taste; lacks charm	ice cream
light	sharp, almost fizzy on tongue; light but earthy flavor	root vegetables
grassy	grassy tasting; tart but not unpleasant; short afterburn	cottage consump-tion
light, flowery	pleasant; good food wine; smooth	veal chops
mild fruit	slightly fruity flavor; very smooth but lacks bite; pleasant	lemon chicken
light, fruity	light, pleasant, and harmonious but a bit flat; smooth pleasant finish	salmon dishes
sharp	burns the tongue; lacks body; epoxy aftertaste	candy floss
blackberries	sweet in the mouth but dry and some-what harsh aftertaste	pork chops and apple sauce
fruity	thin, watery summer plonk*	cottage guests

*A popular term for a quaffing wine with no particular distinctive qualities except its reasonable price. Plonk it down and drink it.

WHITE WINES

REF. NO.	DESCRIPTION	PROVINCES AVAILABLE	RELATIVE SWEETNESS

AMERICAN (continued)

REF. NO.	DESCRIPTION	PROVINCES AVAILABLE	RELATIVE SWEETNESS
009373	Gallo Sauvignon Blanc	BC A M O Q NB NS PEI NFLD	semidry
080192	Guasti French Colombard	M	medium dry
029119	Inglenook French Colombard	BC A S O	moderately sweet
014837	Inglenook Navalle Chenin Blanc	O	sugary
075671	Los Hermanos Chenin Blanc	O	very sweet
086355	Parducci California White	A	sweetish
047399	Paul Masson Chenin Blanc	BC	medium dry
075689	San Martin Chablis	O	dry
023150	Sebastiani Mountain Chablis	BC A S	off dry
075697	Summit Chablis	O	medium dry
075739	Summit Rhine	O	softly sweet
042010	Sutton Hill California French Colombard	BC	medium dry
014928	Vin de la Paix Chablis	O	slightly sweet
080366	Wente Brothers le Blanc de Blancs	A	mildly sweet
047993	Wente Brothers Sauvignon Blanc	A S	dry

BOUQUET	TASTE COMMENTS	SUITABLE WITH
pleasant, fresh and fruity	pleasant but thin, not much body; slightly cloying; bites back	tuna sandwiches
light	bland; astringent; not much flavor	wine spritzers
caramelly	some body; rich and sweet without much balancing acid	sardines
floral	fruity chemical flavor; not unpleasant; kicks back	rice pudding
strong, spicy	full but flat flavor; not bad if you can get past the sweetness	ham steak
light but flavorful	flat and thin; unpleasant aftertaste	windsurfing
strong, fruity	full, fruity, flowery flavor; ripe grape aftertaste	pâté
full, musty	tart, some flavor; drinkable but not much character	shopping malls
flavorful	thin and spineless; no bite; little depth	pound cake
fruity	clean, nutty taste; a bit cloying but a pleasant summer drink served well chilled	lazy summer Sundays
spicy	mellow and fruity; good body; bitter finish spoils the flavor	poultry with fruit stuffing
quite fruity	fruit hidden by acidity; nondescript	egg salad sandwiches
honey nose	pleasant but tired; taste dies quickly	soda for spritzers
flowery	fruity; pleasant quaffing wine; lacks bite; sweetness clings a bit	perogies or other dumplings
lemons	fresh flavor; chalky, astringent aftertaste but nice	veal paillard

WHITE WINES

REF. NO.	DESCRIPTION	PROVINCES AVAILABLE	RELATIVE SWEETNESS

AUSTRALIAN

REF. NO.	DESCRIPTION	PROVINCES AVAILABLE	RELATIVE SWEETNESS
089359	Hardy's Burgundy Blanc	O	dry
069484	Hardy's Saint Vincent Chablis	A O	dry
085142	Kaiser Stuhl Chablis	BC	dry
028076	Kaiser Stuhl Riesling	BC A M O NB	lightly sweet
028274	Kirkton Australian Chablis	BC A	medium dry
040683	Lindeman's Ben Ean Moselle	BC A S M	medium sweet
019596	Lindeman's Cawarra Riesling	BC A	dry with some sweetness
093393	Lindeman's White Burgundy	BC	medium sweet
005231	Porphry Pearl	A	very sweet
055640	Seppelt Muroomba	BC S M O NB NS NFLD	sweetish
033282	Yalumba Four Crown Riesling	BC A S O	dry

AUSTRIAN

REF. NO.	DESCRIPTION	PROVINCES AVAILABLE	RELATIVE SWEETNESS
003855	Blue Danube (Lenz Moser)	BC A S M O Q NB NS PEI NFLD	semisweet
051813	Kremser Jungfrau Spätlese (Krems)	O	medium dry
037556	Kremser Rosengarten (Krems)	M O	dryish
083238	Kremser Schmidt (Krems)	O	dry

BOUQUET	TASTE COMMENTS	SUITABLE WITH
appley	spritzy, thin but acceptable for a picnic	picnics
fruity	thin, watery, a bit of taste; fizzy	unripe kiwis
lingering fruit	slightly effervescent; little body or flavor; like bicarbonate of soda	a headache
faintly fruity	apple cider or ginger ale taste	rye whiskey
negligible	short on flavor and acid; bland	a salt-free diet
flowery, muscat nose	fruity, muscat taste; light and a bit short on bite but has real character	lemon chicken
a bit flowery	not strong; innoffensive; hock-like	cold light dishes
delicate	light but plenty of fruit; some bite; a drinkable everyday wine	quiche
fruity	very sweet on tongue; light but potent; burns going down	cherry jam
smells like a soft drink	fruity, soft, slightly sweet but dries out in your mouth	summer drinking on the beach
smoky	tart, fruity taste; zingy fruitiness disappears quickly	lemon pie
mild, grassy	good tasting sweetish wine of little distinction	apple tart
gardenias	fruity, mellow, and soft; sweet taste lingers; very drinkable	picnics
flowery	light and pleasant; somewhat harsh; a touch of pizazz	a walk in the woods
flowery	full and mellow; a little warm on finish; real character; excellent food wine	salmon in phyllo pastry

WHITE WINES

REF. NO.	DESCRIPTION	PROVINCES AVAILABLE	RELATIVE SWEETNESS
AUSTRIAN (continued)			
131203	Magic Flute (Morandell)	BC A M O NB	fairly dry
040709	Schluck (Lenz Moser)	M O	hint of sweetness
BULGARIAN			
014845	Hemus (Vinimpex)	A S O Q NB NS PEI	semisweet
CANADIAN			
006023	Andres Auberge	S M O NB NS PEI	some sweetness
015776	Andres Cellar Cask Reserve	A S M O	sweetish
087973	Andres Domaine D'Or	BC O	dry
083600	Andres Fiorino	O	semisweet
075838	Andres Franciscan Chablis	BC A O NS	medium to dry
016311	Andres Hochtaler	BC S M O Q NB NS	semidry
088799	Andres Pacific Coast Chablis	BC A S	medium dry
008557	Andres Regency Dry	BC M O NS	semidry
088443	Andres Rhinekeller	O	somewhat sweet
093995	Andres Schloss Wilhelm Riesling	A S M NB NS PEI	sweet
075812	Andres Wintergarten	A S M O	quite sweet
035964	Barnes Bon Appétit	O	medium sweet

BOUQUET	TASTE COMMENTS	SUITABLE WITH
fruity	pleasant, palatable wine; has some fruit but leaves a slightly bitter after-taste	veal with apples
apples with cinnamon	not distinctive; unobtrusive on your palate but drinkable	sweet and sour chicken
revolting	heavy and cloying; flat, sweet taste; unpleasant aftertaste	anchovies
tinny	hint of blackberries; strong, fruity finish	apple betty
missing	disposable bag, disposable wine	dispositions
none	very dry; sour taste; bitter; no flavor; almost undrinkable	grapefruit
musty	thin; cloying aftertaste, grapy	plastic-ware party
pungent	thin, pleasant; drink very chilled; suitable for general quaffing	large groups
mildly fruity	easy drinking, straightforward but dull	brunch
clean, fruity	light, drinkable, decent but not exciting	trout amandine
after shave	quite acidic, with Concord zing aftertaste	unwelcome guests
faintly fruity	fruity and soft with harsh aftertaste but not much flavor	hamburgers
clean, fruity	light, watery, undistinguished; slightly bitter aftertaste	oom pah pah band
full, fruity	very sweet and cloying; thin, inelegant	oatmeal cookies
perfumy	has the flavor of flowery perfume; quite sweetish but quaffable	fruit salad

WHITE WINES

REF. NO.	DESCRIPTION	PROVINCES AVAILABLE	RELATIVE SWEETNESS

CANADIAN (continued)

REF. NO.	DESCRIPTION	PROVINCES AVAILABLE	RELATIVE SWEETNESS
086074	Barnes Heritage Estate Chablis	S M O NFLD	dry
104489	Barnes Heritage Estate Rhine	O	mildly sweet
027276	Barnes Ontario Country	S O	dry musty
079749	Barnes Weinfest	A S M O NS	medium sweet
099838	Brights Baron Ludwig	O	medium sweet
089078	Brights Dry House	BC S O	dry
075853	Brights Entre-Lacs	S M O PEI	dry
001719	Brights House	BC A S M O NB NS PEI NFLD	semisweet
079756	Brights Liebesheim	BC S M O Q PEI	sweet
011247	Brights President Extra Dry	O	off dry
081539	Brights Riuscita	O	sweet
046243	Brights Warnerhof	S M O NB NS	off dry
023267	Chantecler Table Ronde	O Q	semisweet
081596	Charal Chandelle Blanc	O	medium dry
055194	Charal Duchess	O	medium
057158	Charal Seyval Blanc	O	dry

BOUQUET	TASTE COMMENTS	SUITABLE WITH
stale roses	sour, unpleasant; has the flavor of cream soda	mouthwash
lightly foxy	thin candy flavor; smooth aftertaste	candy canes
musty	plenty of fruit but not always the one you want; Concord afterglow, fruity	sardines
caustic soda	tastes O.K. if you hold your nose; grape juice-like	sinus clearing
fruity but not pleasant	watery and thin; mediocre; pleasant aftertaste	a cold
light, almost missing	use only for marinating	marinating flank steak
lightly flowery	light, lacks body; some fruit; a bit flat; slightly bitter aftertaste	hot dogs for lunch
pepperminty, sharp	hint of *labrusca;* fairly well balanced; the taste is more herbal than fruity	lemon chicken
none	bland but very sweet; not enough acid; hint of peppermint; innoffensive	Nanaimo bars
slightly flowery	smooth, straightforward; a bit stale; warm finish; not much depth	turkey sandwiches
pearlike	slightly fizzy on tongue; white grape juice; no finish	peanut butter sandwiches
winy	bitter taste at first which smooths out	fried chicken
fermenting peach nectar	initially biting, then flabby; poor aftertaste	an argument
full, fruity	loads of taste and depth; has some character; aftertaste a bit sweet	barbecued shrimp
apples	candy apple taste but watery and flat	melons at brunch
light, fruity	a little sharp at first but grows on you; pleasant, acceptable	fresh cheese

WHITE WINES

REF. NO.	DESCRIPTION	PROVINCES AVAILABLE	RELATIVE SWEETNESS

CANADIAN (continued)

REF. NO.	DESCRIPTION	PROVINCES AVAILABLE	RELATIVE SWEETNESS
056754	Château des Charmes Chardonnay	O NS	dry
079707	Château des Charmes Cour Blanc	O NFLD	medium sweet
081570	Château des Charmes Nokara Chardonnay	O	dry
081562	Château des Charmes Nokara Riesling	O	lightly sweet
061499	Château des Charmes Riesling	O	dry
057455	Château des Charmes Sentinel	A M O	moderately dry
049544	Château des Charmes Seyval Blanc	O	dry
000950	Château-Gai Alpenweiss	BC A S M O Q NB NS PEI NFLD	medium sweet
010561	Château-Gai Cartier Canadian Riesling	O	dryish
087254	Château-Gai Chianno Bianco	A O NB	medium sweet
075754	Château-Gai Edelwein	BC A S M O NB NS PEI	semisweet
081612	Château-Gai Johannisberg Riesling	BC A M O	medium
081604	Château-Gai Pinot Chardonnay	O	dry
079723	Château-Gai Princière	O NB NFLD	dry
093559	Claremont Riesling	BC	semisweet
082792	Colio Bianco	S O	semisweet

BOUQUET	TASTE COMMENTS	SUITABLE WITH
faint, musty, fruity	medium body; agreeable flavor that lasts; plenty of bite	shrimp or eggs
hint of nail polish remover	some fruit; poor finish; watery; one sip is enough	cafeteria food
lightly fruity; yeasty	slightly yeasty at first; some nutty flavor; hot on the palate	trout amandine
fruit that fades	good flavor; tart and tasty; sweetish but not cloying on finish	summer picnics
strong, sharp	musty taste at first, pleasant flavor follows; fruity and pleasant	raclette
caramelly	pleasant but taste gets lost; nondescript	brunch
pungent	tasty but somewhat flat; a little rough; acceptable	asparagus with hollandaise
slightly pungent	some bite but basically bland; lingering foxy flavor; acidic	fish sticks
Concord grape	pepperminty; a bit of a rough taste	after-dinner mints
musty	cloying but not all bad	perfect spritzer base
candylike	bitter, cloying; tingly aftertaste	a trip up the Rhine
spicy, fruity	light and tasty but doesn't live up to its nose; a bit flat but still enjoyable	smoked fish
light, flowery	light but firm taste; delicate, fresh; some flavor and complexity	chicken in a pot
chemical	no taste, no class	no food
honey nose	fresh and grapy but a bit harsh; plenty of bite; odd aftertaste	sweetbreads
herbal but harsh	intense herbal initial taste but clumsy hot aftertaste; acceptable	peaches in wine

WHITE WINES

REF. NO.	DESCRIPTION	PROVINCES AVAILABLE	RELATIVE SWEETNESS
CANADIAN (continued)			
079814	Colio Bianco Secco	S O	dry but not bone dry
089284	Colio Perla	O	quite sweet
010231	Géloso Cuvée Blanc	O Q	dry
088344	Grand Patron	O	dry
006700	Inniskillin Brae Blanc	A S M O PEI NFLD	dry
083790	Inniskillin Riesling	O NS	dry with a sweet edge
076125	Inniskillin Seyval Blanc	O	medium dry
079780	Inniskillin Vidal	O	off dry
078402	Jordan Falkenberg	BC A M O NB	moderately dry
079681	Jordan Grande Cuvée	O	dry with sweet overtones
006411	Jordan Maria Christina	BC A S M O NB NS PEI NFLD	medium sweet
006007	Jordan Rhinecastle	S M O NS PEI NFLD	medium sweet
086199	Jordan Sainte Michelle Johannisberg Riesling	BC	very sweet
080655	Jordan Selected Riesling	O	moderately sweet
010686	Jordan Toscano	BC A S O	off dry

BOUQUET	TASTE COMMENTS	SUITABLE WITH
light, pleasant	well balanced; plenty of fruit and acid; gives impression of potential; drinkable	guacamole
caustic soda	fizzy and sweet; a stomach cleaner	a hangover
ether	flabby and thin; bland, astringent; overtones of green apples	a toothache
fresh, flowery	thin but enough body to drink with food; clean, little character	fish and chips
light with a hint of grape	dry, short; slightly sickly aftertaste	chicken salad
slightly yeasty	pleasant but a bitter flavor which lingers; plenty of bite; a good Riesling with food	prosciutto and melon
fruity	quite light; tart but pleasing; somewhat bland	sole
fruity	mellow fruitiness; needs more bite but very pleasant	meringues
musty	foxy flavor dominates; light and acidic; ordinary	tuna casserole
fruity	bitterness comes through except for the sweetness at the end	breaking up
pungent, fruity	sweetish taste; slightly harsh finish; similar to apple cider	apple pie
faintly fruity	thin; clings to the mouth	young love
pleasant, flowery	poignant; lots of fruit; well balanced; nice afterburn	a picnic in the park
spring blossoms	very light; quite sweet with pro- nounced floral flavor; warm aftertaste	home video
distinctive piny, unnatural	grapefruity but smooth; slightly cloying aftertaste; like sweet pear nectar	picnics and pine cones

WHITE WINES

REF. NO.	DESCRIPTION	PROVINCES AVAILABLE	RELATIVE SWEETNESS
CANADIAN (continued)			
026195	Mission Hill Chablis	BC	medium sweet
101774	Mission Hill Chenin Blanc	BC	quite sweet
104158	Mission Hill Gewurztraminer	BC	fairly sweet
104141	Mission Hill Johan-nisberg Riesling	BC	medium sweet
100024	Mission Hill Premium White	BC	medium dry
101808	Pandosy Country White	BC	medium dry
023267	Rêve d'été (Société des alcools du Québec)	O Q	dry with touch of sweetness
104349	Ridout Château-Gai Chablis	A	medium dry
104364	Ridout Château-Gai Rhine	A	sweet
020573	Sainte Michelle Chenin Blanc	BC S M	moderately sweet
082818	Villa Cusato	O	semidry
CHILEAN			
075721	Oro Del Rhin (Conch Y Toro)	BC O	fairly dry
FRENCH			
036913	Alsace Coquillages (Trimbach)	A Q	dry
005967	Anjou (Remy-Pannier)	BC A S M O Q NB	fairly dry

BOUQUET	TASTE COMMENTS	SUITABLE WITH
interesting, fruity	enjoyable sweet flavor; distinctive	banana splits
quite fruity	sweetish on tongue; light and pleasant; sweetness stays with you; quite average	afternoon snacks
green grapes	sweet, spicy flavor lingers on the tongue; a bit thin, almost diluted	salmon terrine
touch of licorice	plenty of bite but flavor lost in overwhelming sweetness; mellow finish	shrimp with Pernod
mild, fairly pleasant	fruity flavor; some bitterness under the sweetness	sweet potatoes
almost missing	light, pleasant and undistinguished; promising but needs more strength	limp asparagus
faint	harsh but lots of flavor; plenty of depth; lacks acid; flavor a bit tainted	choucroute garni
very light	lacks a defined taste; faint Concord glow	making grape jelly
faint scent	light, watery; sweet, chalky finish but not totally unacceptable	picnics in the mountains
very faint, flowery	light, mild and pleasant; shallow but sippable	a summer storm
fruity	not enough taste but palatable; pleasant drinking especially for untutored palates	simple food
faintly fruity	bouquet is the high point; toothpaste aftertaste	mouthwash
faint, woody	some flavor and depth; drinks easily	scallops in Pernod
pleasant	mellow, soft, good drinking; good before dinner	hors d'oeuvres

WHITE WINES

REF. NO.	DESCRIPTION	PROVINCES AVAILABLE	RELATIVE SWEETNESS

FRENCH (continued)

REF. NO.	DESCRIPTION	PROVINCES AVAILABLE	RELATIVE SWEETNESS
055178	Anjou Blanc (de Neuville)	M O	slightly sweet
040329	Beau-Rivage (Borie-Manoux)	A O	off dry
039172	Beauchoisy (Chapin & Landais)	O Q	dry
010884	Blanc de Blancs (Calvet)	BC O	dry
075390	Blanc de Blancs (Chantovent)	O	tart, sweetish edge
026195	Blanc de Blancs (La Marinière)	BC A	fairly dry
075358	Blanc de Blancs (Remy-Pannier)	O	slightly sweet
016923	Bordeaux (Dumons)	O NFLD	dry
087742	Bourgogne Aligote (Ropiteau)	A O	dry
067835	Canteval (Nicolas)	O	dry
092206	Château Arnaud Jouan Premières (Dourthe Frères)	Q	very sweet
083709	Château Bonnet Entre-Deux-Mers	O	fairly dry
080168	Château Branda (Giraud)	S M	dryish
104034	Château Lamote (Lichine)	O	dry
045328	Coteaux du Layon (Remy-Pannier)	A	sweet

BOUQUET	TASTE COMMENTS	SUITABLE WITH
almond essence	sweetish with tart edges; appley finish fills the mouth	almond tart
flinty	light, lots of bite; not much fruit; soft finish; acceptable	pasta with white sauce
mild but pleasant	acidic, hint of grapefruit; not much flavor	ice cubes
pleasant but light	well balanced with some character; easy drinking	mushrooms in cream
some fruit	tart, very acidic with a sweetish finish; not much flavor but good plonk	onion soup
slightly yeasty	strong, somewhat earthy flavor; unpleasant aftertaste	Greek food
very soft	watery but pleasant; nice bite; doesn't offend	drinks before dinner
faint, bitter	fizzy on the tongue; light green apple flavor; lacks bite but certainly drinkable	quiche
thin, acidic	some bite; fruity and pleasant; bitter aftertaste; unspectacular	tuna salad
light	straightforward light blend; touch of sweetness	bagels and cream cheese
syrupy; honey nose	cloying; syrupy, medicinal; some oxidation evident	desserts
pronounced fruit on nose	interesting, earthy character but thin with bitter finish; doesn't live up to bouquet	ham sandwiches
under-developed	coarse, young wine; some bite but harsh; could improve with age	Sichuan fish
light	dry, fresh, delicate, and subtle	shellfish
mild, grapey	quite sweet and oily; lacks bite and flavor but easy to drink	Greek pastries

WHITE WINES

REF. NO.	DESCRIPTION	PROVINCES AVAILABLE	RELATIVE SWEETNESS

FRENCH (continued)

REF. NO.	DESCRIPTION	PROVINCES AVAILABLE	RELATIVE SWEETNESS
075416	Côtes du Duras (Chauvenet)	S O NFLD	dryish
073254	Côtes du Rhône (Mommessin)	O	nice and dry
081885	Côtes du Rhône Prieure Saint Julien	Q	dry
035667	Crystal d'Alsace (Dopff & Irion)	O Q NS	dry
091645	Cuvée de Patriot Blanc (Société des alcools du Québec)	Q	dry
041657	Cuvée Jean Calvet (Calvet)	O	dry
036582	Cuvée les Amours (Hugel)	Q	medium dry
099960	Cuvée Madame (Bichot)	O Q NB PEI	dry
054890	Cuvée Spéciale (Barton & Guestier)	BC O NB NS PEI	dry
082800	De Marbrier Domain Saint Martin	Q	slightly sweet
046318	Entre-Deux-Mers (Dumons)	O	dry
041285	Entre-Deux-Mers (Paul Bouchard)	O	very dry
011981	Entre-Deux-Mers (Schröder & Schyler)	BC M O NB PEI NFLD	dry
075333	Entre-Deux-Mers (Triton)	BC S M O	dry
092312	Entre-Deux-Mers Château de Goëlane (Ets. Castel Frères)	Q	dry

BOUQUET	TASTE COMMENTS	SUITABLE WITH
light, fruity	a bit harsh on the palate but has some depth of flavor; slight sweetness lingers	nibblies
lightly fruity	tingles on your tongue; good dry aftertaste; lingers well	barbecued shrimp
flowery, fine	soft but biting; a gentle wine; interesting taste but not much of it	poached chicken breasts
faint, grapey odor	crisp and "spritzig", a little fruit; pleasant enough	fish
faint	light style but watery and no depth; water is cheaper	ice cubes
imperceptible	bland but passable; not special	chicken wings
fruity	quite acidic; appley; finishes fairly long	fish soup
candylike	the sharpness overcomes the flavor	fish curry
innocuous	fruity at the front; dry and acidic at the back; a neutral wine	basic bistro fare
light	perfumy taste; pleasant, light; taste lingers but you wish it wouldn't	perfume
light, fruity	not much taste; rough and harsh; a young wine	vegetable curry
flinty fruit	crisp, tart with some fruit; sound wine for light food	fish with cream sauce
full, appley aroma	tart, appley; pleasant fruity aftertaste; a good food wine	prawns and avocado
pleasant, fruity	tart and tasty; drinkable plonk	fish
neutral, faint licorice odor	insipid; watery; generally lacking in all areas	nothing

WHITE WINES

REF. NO.	DESCRIPTION	PROVINCES AVAILABLE	RELATIVE SWEETNESS

FRENCH (continued)

REF. NO.	DESCRIPTION	PROVINCES AVAILABLE	RELATIVE SWEETNESS
026674	Entre-Deux-Mers La Gamage (Rineau)	Q	dry
075366	Gaillac (Paul Bouchard)	A O	dry
052340	Grand Seigneur (Poulet)	O Q	dry
040972	Graves (Cruse)	A M O NB NFLD	very dry
013235	Graves (N. Vernaux)	Q	very dry
099127	Gros Plant du Pays	Q	very dry
021790	La Bordelaise (Loudenne)	A M O NB	dry
020628	La Cour Pavillon (Loudenne)	BC A S M O Q NB NFLD	dry
051136	Le Gamine (Hasenklever)	O	dry
091728	Le Girondin Bordeaux	Q	dry
059568	Le Piat D'Or (Piat)	BC A M O NB NFLD	dryish
042473	L'Epayrie (Roux)	BC O Q NB NS PEI	dry
004226	Lion D'Or (Calvet)	A M O NS	slightly sweet
027532	Louis XIV Sauvignon (Johnston)	O	dry
052092	Mommessin Export (Mommessin)	S O NFLD	dry

BOUQUET	TASTE COMMENTS	SUITABLE WITH
honeyed complex nose; attractive	does not follow through in mouth; unbalanced; acidic; short	seafood
faintly fruity	flat and harsh; not much flavor; unripe, unready, and probably never will be	snuff
fruity but very light	slightly bitter; flavor fades; quite light; acceptable	simple food
fruity; very good	fresh, flinty taste; subtle and delicate	sole bonne femme
austere; nondescript	overacidic; fairly long with musty finish	fish
sea spray nose	acidity overpowering; no discernible fruit	rich seafood
light, fresh	musty edge at first; astringent; lacks charm	baked fish
light	not enough grape; bittersweet; green	cod
fruity	strong bite hides taste; bitter after-taste, bites back	fried smelts
a little musty	very dry, almost arid; light but not refreshing	desert songs
light, mellow	some body; touch of sweetness on the tongue; smooth finish	leek tarts
apples and flowers	good initial flavor but fades away	barbecued fish
fruity	straightforward, pleasant; slightly sweet on the tongue; leaves a fond memory	home cooking
light, subtle	thin with some bite; pleasant aftertaste; ordinary	cheese omelet
faint, appley	tart, some flavor; goes down easily; palatable	Sunday dinners

WHITE WINES

REF. NO.	DESCRIPTION	PROVINCES AVAILABLE	RELATIVE SWEETNESS

FRENCH (continued)

REF. NO.	DESCRIPTION	PROVINCES AVAILABLE	RELATIVE SWEETNESS
040741	Monbazillac (S.I.C.A.)	Q	medium sweet
060517	Moreau Blanc (Moreau)	BC A S M O Q NB PEI NFLD	dry
002527	Mouton-Cadet Blanc (P. de Rothschild)	BC A S M O Q NB NS PEI NFLD	dry
013821	Muscadet (Remy-Pannier)	BC M O Q NB	dry
093815	Muscadet Wine Guild	M O	very dry
086751	Olivier de France Bordeaux Blanc (Eschenauer)	O NS	dryish
101352	Partager Vin Blanc (Barton & Guestier)	S M	dry
002535	Prince Blanc (Barton & Guestier)	M O Q NB NS PEI	dry
079665	Prince de Galles (Chapin & Landais)	O	dry
029918	Roc Blanc (Cruse)	O	dryish
026708	Saint Jovian Blanc de Blancs (Yvon Mau)	BC S O Q	medium
060160	Sauvignon de Touraine	Q	dry
001164	Sélection (Kressmann)	BC A S M O NB NS PEI NFLD	vaguely dry
099549	Vin de France (Lichine)	O	dry
050161	Vouvray Chenin Blanc	BC	medium dry

BOUQUET	TASTE COMMENTS	SUITABLE WITH
clean, grapey; honeyed tones	good acid to balance out sweetness; does not cloy on palate; nice aftertaste	desserts, chicken livers
faintly acidic	very tart, makes your mouth pucker; lacks body; not much flavor	chicken curry
fruity	light but sharp on the tongue; some fruit; bitter aftertaste	chicken in cream sauce
light, fruity	mild and pleasant; appley; well balanced but innocuous	white fish
light, fruity	tart but not much behind it; pleasant, slightly bitter aftertaste	fish pâté
like grape-fruit	mild, pleasant, slightly grapefruity taste; short	pork chops
summery	flinty, dry and pleasant; well balanced; slight bitterness in the finish	salmon in phyllo pastry
faint, not too pleasant	some fruit, some taste but fleeting	chicken salad
flowery, fine	soft but biting; a gentle wine; interesting taste but not much of it	poached chicken breasts
soft	mellow and soft; easy drinking; good for brunches or showers when a tipple is wanted	cheese dreams
tries hard to come through	thin; some flavor but it disappears quickly	mild cheese
medicinal	excessive acidity; watery	very sharp cheese
fresh, light	fruity and clean but uninteresting	chicken in a pot
smooth, light, fruity	light, fruit flavor; straightforward and tasty	poached eggs
fruity	young and fresh; subtle flavor; elegant	fruit and cheese

WHITE WINES

REF. NO.	DESCRIPTION	PROVINCES AVAILABLE	RELATIVE SWEETNESS

GERMAN

REF. NO.	DESCRIPTION	PROVINCES AVAILABLE	RELATIVE SWEETNESS
086314	Alsheimer Rheinblick (Kendermman)	A	moderately sweet
086322	Bechtheimer Pilgerfad (Zimmermann-Graef)	A	quite sweet
036111	Bereich Beernkastel Bishop of Riesling (Rudolph Muller)	BC A M O	medium sweet
011098	Bereich Bernkastel Kellerprinz (F. Reh)	A S O	medium sweet
043885	Bereich Nierstein Domprinz (F. Reh)	O	semisweet
077677	Bereich Nierstein Fisherman (G.A. Schmitt)	BC A S M O	off dry
073783	Bereich Wonnegau Erben Spätlese (Langguth)	A	off dry
015875	Beernkasteler Kurfurstlay Riesling	A M	medium sweet
016386	Black Forest Girl (Z.B.W.)	BC A S M O NS PEI NFLD	semisweet
070003	Deinhock (Deinhard)	O	medium sweet
047399	Father Rhine Rhinewine	BC	moderately sweet
069740	Forellenwein (Deinhard)	O	off dry
035758	Goldener Weinberg (Hoch)	O	quite sweet
080275	Graacher Munzlay (Kendermann)	A	medium dry
020495	Green Gold Riesling (Kendermann)	BC A S M O Q NB	moderately dry

BOUQUET	TASTE COMMENTS	SUITABLE WITH
musty	fruity and sweetish; lacks bite; bland but acceptable	party sandwiches
full flavored	good sweet wine; plenty of flavor; full bodied; sweetness clings	cheesecake
muted, flowery	medium body; quite sweet but sweetness balanced by acid; sweetness clings a little	a casual afternoon
fruity	thin but tart for a sweet wine; fades to nothing	summer food
light	smooth and pleasant; not exciting; fruity	dull company
light, fruity	lots of taste; fruit and flavor lasts; sweetish aftertaste; quite good	fashion shows
flavorful	pleasant, round body; very fruity with light lingering aftertaste	*strudel mit shlag*
heady	softy and mellow; smooth flavor	brunch
very fruity	clumsy, cloying finish; bad imitation of a good German wine	lots of soda, lemon, and ice
very fruity	sweet but well balanced; fruity finish; pleasant	scallops in wine
full, fruity	some flavor and bite; fruit shows through the sweetness; pleasant quaffing wine	tennis
fruity	light and fresh; sweetness clings a little; drinkable	scallops
faint	sweet with lots of tang; warm, sweet aftertaste	weekend friends
fruity	fruity; clean; relatively light and pleasant	casual drinking
light, pleasant	some body; balanced, fruity taste but flavor doesn't last	pears and brie

WHITE WINES

REF. NO.	DESCRIPTION	PROVINCES AVAILABLE	RELATIVE SWEETNESS

GERMAN (continued)

REF. NO.	DESCRIPTION	PROVINCES AVAILABLE	RELATIVE SWEETNESS
026567	Hambacher Riesling (Hoch)	O	medium dry
054163	Johannisberger Erntebrenger (Kendermann)	A	sweet
086330	Kaiserstuhl-Tuniberg (Z.B.W.)	A	medium dry
067389	Konzert Trocken (Schroll & Hillebrand)	BC A O	moderately dry
032631	Liebfraumilch (Drathen)	O	fairly dry
000729	Liebfraumilch Blue Nun (Sichel)	O	moderately sweet
018432	Liebfraumilch Crown of Crowns	BC A S M O Q NB NS PEI NFLD	medium sweet
005769	Liebfraumilch Madonna (Valckenberg)	BC A S M O Q	slightly sweet
028340	Liebfraumilch Rhinekeller	BC A S M O Q NB NS PEI NFLD	medium
028282	Liebfraumilch Wedding Veil	BC S M O PEI	mildly sweet
018002	Moselmaid (Deinhard)	A S O NS PEI NFLD	quite sweet
069872	Müller-Thurgau (Deinhard)	O	sweet
033720	Niersteiner Gutes Domtal (Brosch)	BC A	semidry
069559	Night Music (Rosenhof)	S M O NB NS NFLD	moderately sweet
080259	Ockfener Bockstein (H. Schmitt)	A M	medium dry

BOUQUET	TASTE COMMENTS	SUITABLE WITH
faintly fruity	light and sweet but well balanced; quite nice; a bit short on the finish	vanilla ice cream
minty	clear and refreshing; lots of bite but not much flavor	veal stew
mildly fruity	tangy but no life	candy kisses
some fruit	good fruit with bite; short on taste	mineral water
yeasty	a quaffing wine of no great distinction	B.Y.O.B. parties
light	heavy, almost oily texture, clean finish; no persistence	potato salad
delicate	very fruity; has an elegant touch	pastries in the afternoon
earthy	flat pop; smooth finish	chips and dip
pleasant	light and pleasant; easy to drink	sautéed fish
mild, fruity	mellow but diluted taste	spring sunshine
not much	plenty of fruit and acid; some depth of flavor; sweet aftertaste; good drinking	good times
faintly fruity	no faults but not much character	dull conversation
flowery	light wine; lots of glycerine	pool, patio, or picnic
sour	a mouthful of fruit; much better than smell	fresh strawberries
faint but clean	clean, good fruit and acid balance but no pizazz	squash

WHITE WINES

REF. NO.	DESCRIPTION	PROVINCES AVAILABLE	RELATIVE SWEETNESS
GERMAN (continued)			
042713	Piesporter Michels-berg (Drathen)	O	quite sweet
038018	Rudesheimer Rosen-garten (Kendermann)	O	moderately sweet
035030	Saint Johanner Abtey (H. Schmitt)	A O	medium sweet
030510	Senator's Rhine (Sichel)	S O	moderately sweet
035089	Weinheimer Sybillenstein (Racke)	M O	quite sweet
029157	Wiltinger Scharzberg Zentral	O	sweet
062745	Zeller Grafschaft (Kurfurstliche)	A	slightly sweet
043505	Zeller Schwarze Katz (Sichel)	BC A S M NB NS NFLD	medium sweet
GREEK			
053918	Apelia (Courtakis)	BC M O NS PEI	dry
085514	Apollo (Courtakis)	O	dry, almost bitter
HUNGARIAN			
005405	Badacsonyi Szur-kebarat (Monimpex)	BC A S M O Q NB NS PEI NFLD	softly dry
010439	Debroi Harslevelu (Monimpex)	BC A M O Q	sweet tinge
000836	Jaszberenyi Rizling (Monimpex)	BC M O Q NB NS PEI	dry
ISRAEL			
029041	Carmel French Colombard	O NFLD	semidry

BOUQUET	TASTE COMMENTS	SUITABLE WITH
lightly fragrant	rich peachlike flavor which lasts; sweetness offset by acid which burns palate	peach tart with cream
fruity	plenty of acid and fruit; flavor persists, good finish	orange mousse
full, aromatic	light bodied; full of taste; not exciting	apple torte
very light	spiked pineapple juice; flat	bad mornings
fruity	lots of fruit; very pleasant; relatively sweet with dry finish	a stroll by the river
full, smooth	delicately balanced; some depth of flavor with plenty of acid to offset the sweetness	elegant lunches
truffles	full of flavor, well balanced; enjoyable	backyard aperitifs
a whiff of fruit	thin, watery; not much taste; forgettable before it's finished	meatloaf sandwiches
innocuous	drinkable but watery; some tartness	taramosalata
sharp but faint resin odor	acidic; sour apple taste but a redeeming flavor creeps in	chicken kabob
musky	fruity, full of taste; lots of flavor and softness	barbecued shrimp
under-whelming	slightly fruity; relatively smooth; no afterburn; lots of earthy flavor	chicken paprikash
earthy	bitter; harsh; draws your taste buds together but smooths out	office Christmas parties
delicate	round with some body; very drinkable; smooth	roast chicken

WHITE WINES

REF. NO.	DESCRIPTION	PROVINCES AVAILABLE	RELATIVE SWEETNESS

ISRAEL (continued)

| 015081 | Carmel Hock | A O Q | slightly dry |
| 067942 | Carmel Sauvignon Blanc | M O NFLD | dry |

ITALIAN

082628	Biancofiore (Umberto)	O	dry
010207	Castelli Romani (Vini di Velletri)	A O	dry
000711	Colli Albani	BC A S M O Q NB NS PEI NFLD	dry
083758	Cortese di Gavi (Duca d'Asti)	O	dry
046821	Donini Vino di Verona (Lamberti)	BC A S M O Q NB NS PEI NFLD	mildly dry
075523	Dragani Bianco d'Abruzzo	O	dry
079285	Drepano Bianco (Alcamo)	O	dry
075481	Ducale (Chiarli)	O	medium dry
079020	Frascati Superiore (Marino)	O	dry, hint of sweetness
003640	Gambellara (Zonin)	O	dryish
075457	Giacondi (Cierrevi)	BC A S M O NB NS PEI NFLD	slightly sweet
079038	Lacrima d'Arno (Melini)	M O	dry

BOUQUET	TASTE COMMENTS	SUITABLE WITH
powerful fruit, chemical grape	doesn't appear to resemble a wine; ginger ale flavor	rye
dull	insipid; bitter aftertaste; unimpressive	matzoh balls
light	leaves a slight fizz on the tongue; tangy but dull	lasagna
very light	sharp candylike flavor; astringent	peanut butter cups
non-existent	harsh initially; a bit flat; watery	student life
sweet at first, then dry	sweet but stinging aftertaste; not much foretaste	antipasto
crisp	crisp, light, some flavor with smooth finish	veal chops
dull, nondescript	touch of sweetness; nice tang; not much to it; fades quickly	fried rice
hint of grape	pleasant but dull, even boring; lacks bite	yesterday's gossip
wet fur, musty	fizzy and sharp; medicinal	marinade
fruity, even flowery	soft and fruity; very pleasant; easy drinking	veal Orloff
very faint	watery; sharp but not unpleasant; some taste comes through	chicken and almonds
hard to pick up	very unassuming; unremarkable; short aftertaste	macaroni and cheese
faint sulphur	light; hardly any taste, bite, or fruit	hot canapés

WHITE WINES

REF. NO.	DESCRIPTION	PROVINCES AVAILABLE	RELATIVE SWEETNESS
ITALIAN (continued)			
069823	Marino (Marino)	O	semidry
031062	Orvieto (Ruffino)	A O PEI NFLD	dry
027698	Orvieto Classico (Melini)	BC S M O Q	semidry
052308	Orvieto Classico (Secco)	S O Q NS	dry
063628	Pinot Bianco (Fontanafredda)	O	bone dry
037366	Pinot Bianco (Ponte)	O	dry
033340	Pinot Grigio (Collavani)	BC M O NB	dry
080762	Prego (S.A.B.R.I.)	O	medium dry
070755	Riunite (Banfi)	A S M O NS PEI NFLD	sweetish
086280	San Grato Lugana (Premiovini)	A	dry
015590	Soave (Negrar)	O	dry
086462	Soave Classico (Fabiano)	O	dry
025007	Soave Classico Superiore (Bertani)	Q	dry
049767	Tocai Friulano (Casarsa)	BC M O	dry
043976	Tocai Friulano (Valle)	M O Q	off dry
067520	Toscano Bianco (Ruffino)	A M	dry
079053	Trebbiano della Toscana (Lamberti)	O PEI	slightly sweet

BOUQUET	TASTE COMMENTS	SUITABLE WITH
alcoholic	sweetish on the tongue; little taste; pleasant finish	linguine with cream sauce
lightly fruity	light, some flavor but slips away	picnics
light	soft, mellow; slightly sweet, good length; a good food wine	peaches in white wine
harsh	raw, harsh; no freshness	green salad
flowery	firm, flavorful; packs lots of power	sole meunière or any good fish dish
delicate, fruity	clean and flavorful; slightly tart; long finish	chicken cacciatore
fruity	very fruity flavor with some body; a tasty wine	veal and mozzarella
light	lightly earthy; some body; decent flavor	chicken pot pie
earthy	fizzy and rough; plenty of fruit; sweetness lingers; not pleasant	junk food dinners
mild, pungent	fresh and light; sound, clear wine without much flavor	pasta carbonara
bland, appley	mouthful of fruit with lots of bite; a lively wine	smoked fish
faint	has some bite and taste; can stand up to strongly flavored food	Chinese food
faint but elegant	sharp taste at first; slight fizz; pleasant, inoffensive flavor; pretty good	pizza with mushrooms
faint, grassy	tart; well balanced but not much charm or personality	scrambled eggs
fruity	straw-colored; some flavor; lacks zest	chicken and chips
reticent	approaches a real wine but has some harshness	pork sausages
faint but fragrant	nippy assertive flavor but little fruit; strong, oxidized	dinner with your mother-in-law

WHITE WINES

REF. NO.	DESCRIPTION	PROVINCES AVAILABLE	RELATIVE SWEETNESS

ITALIAN (continued)

070441	Val d'Adige (Vaja)	BC M O Q NB	dry
069807	Velletri (Co. Pro. Vi.)	A M O	semidry
024422	Verdicchio (Fazi-Battaglia)	A O	dry
037804	Verduzzo (Casarsa)	O	dry
082230	Villa Ambra (Fabiano)	O	semidry
006890	Vino del Veneto (Montresor)	O	dry

NEW ZEALAND

022533	Corban Liebestraum	BC A M O	medium sweet
039958	Corban Sylvaner Riesling	BC A M O	slightly sweet

PORTUGUESE

075663	Vinho Verde (Alianca)	O Q	somewhat sweet

SOUTH AFRICAN

005975	Bonne Esperance	BC A M O NB NS PEI NFLD	dry
064477	Fleur du Cap Emerald Stein	BC M O	medium dry
064659	Grunberger Stein	A	medium dry
913855	Montpellier Chenin Blanc	A	dry

BOUQUET	TASTE COMMENTS	SUITABLE WITH
nil	zesty with some taste; light and refreshing	spinach soufflé
sharp	bland, watery, bitter; vinegary	salad dressing
light	tart; a little fizzy; some flavor; interesting bottle	scallops
faint	flat, watery; not much depth of flavor; dull	fish soup
faint	good, clean taste of fruit; slightly bitter aftertaste	nibblies
light, bland	some freshness; some but not much flavor; boring but acceptable for everyday drinking	stuffed baked potatoes
minimal	flat, unassuming; somewhat acidic in the finish	a Viennese waltz
faint	light with tinge of fruitiness; mild; will never offend	prospective in-laws
old sneakers	very sharp; stale flavor, like moldy ginger ale	tennis
harsh	fizzy; harsh; very acidic; barely an everyday wine	french fries
slight fruit	initially slightly sweet; bitter after-taste; fruity flavor comes through	chicken in peanut sauce
smooth, fruity	a light wine with a fruity bite; pleasant flavor much stronger than bouquet indicates	chicken crêpes
missing and presumed lost	strong initial flavor; somewhat applelike, that lasts; fresh and good	delicate hors d'oeuvres

WHITE WINES

REF. NO.	DESCRIPTION	PROVINCES AVAILABLE	RELATIVE SWEETNESS

SOUTH AFRICAN (continued)

080044	Nederburg Stein	BC M	medium sweet
018689	Paarl Chenin Blanc	BC A M O NB NFLD	medium dry
009878	Paarl Late Vintage	A S M O NB PEI	sweet
006833	Paarl Riesling	BC A M O NS PEI	dryish

SPANISH

082669	Carasol (Santiago)	O	very dry
036822	Marques de Riscal	BC O	dry
016642	Montelorca	M O	off dry
091595	Perce-Neige (Société des alcools du Québec)	Q	dry
092031	Queberac (Société des alcools du Québec)	Q	sweetish
083774	Raimat Can Casal (Coniusa)	O	dry
034447	Rocamar Sarda (Amigo)	M O Q NS	medium dry
047001	San Valentine (Torres)	S M NS	medium dry
020479	Siglo Rioja (Age)	M Q NB	dry
062943	Vina Carossa	O Q	dryish
073106	Vina Esmeralda (Torres)	M	medium dry

BOUQUET	TASTE COMMENTS	SUITABLE WITH
indistinct	young, promising, fruity; a bit puckery	poolside guzzling
slight hint of yeast	fruity, some bite; light body; pleasant	a summer picnic
fragrant	syrupy and rich with a fresh acidic tang; flavor lasts; sweet aftertaste	birthday cake
herbal	taste is there but a bit flat; short on bite	chicken breasts
pungent but pleasant	harsh in the mouth; watery, astringent	broiled fish
pungent	bitter at first but smooths out; the taste is hiding; light, almost watery	leftover leftovers
pleasant, honeyish	plenty of flavor, not lively; mellow and clean aftertaste	gazpacho
almonds	thin and bland but bites back; some fruit	sardine sandwiches
faint, chemical smell	pleasant drinking; sweetish wine	summer sunshine
crisp but some off odors	smooth and well rounded; some depth; decent	Spanish omelet
delicate	flat, unattractive; disappointing after-bouquet; lacks freshness	nothing
soft, subtle	interesting, mild drinking wine; palatable	mild summer evenings
a touch sulphuric	a wine of little character or taste	nothing
almost vegetable-like aroma	has a candy-like taste; slightly fizzy on tongue; vaguely pleasant	cheese fondue
young	harsh taste; not lively	sour grapes

WHITE WINES

REF. NO.	DESCRIPTION	PROVINCES AVAILABLE	RELATIVE SWEETNESS

SPANISH (continued)

| 028035 | Vina Sol (Torres) | BC A M O Q NFLD | dryish |
| 081992 | Yago White (Santiago) | BC A S M O Q NB PEI NFLD | dry |

YUGOSLAVIAN

018903	Muskatni Silvanec (Slovin)	M O	semisweet
009548	Riesling Fruska Gora (Navip)	BC A M O NB	off dry
034090	Riesling Karlovci (Navip)	O	fairly dry
012294	Tiger Milk (Slovin)	M O NB	sweetish
045229	Traminac (Navip)	BC O	off dry
028167	Zilavka Mostar (Hepok)	A O Q	dryish

BOUQUET	TASTE COMMENTS	SUITABLE WITH
fruity, clean	light and fruity; hint of sweetness; good all-purpose wine; definitely drinkable	broiled fish
almost non-existent	steely flavor; hint of fresh-cut grass; a bit harsh but acceptable	paella
musty	tastes like soda pop; acidic aftertaste	nothing
light chemical aroma	dull; not much flavor; strong after-taste; worn out	summer sun by the sea
slightly musky	somewhat harsh but has a pleasant, nutty flavor	clams with garlic
light, fruity	nondescript initial flavor; taste fades quickly; odd, unpleasant aftertaste	patio snacks
flowery	spicy flavor with a little sweetness; round and firm and good tasting	fish soup
stale	woody, chemical; tastes like an imitation wine; burnt out	the morning after

RED WINES

REF. NO.	DESCRIPTION	PROVINCES AVAILABLE	RELATIVE SWEETNESS

AMERICAN

REF. NO.	DESCRIPTION	PROVINCES AVAILABLE	RELATIVE SWEETNESS
065912	Almaden Cabernet Sauvignon	A	dry
0460904	Almaden Zinfandel	A Q	dry
032755	Almaden Mountain Red Burgundy	A S M O PEI	medium dry
048017	Almaden Pinot Noir	A	dry
081422	Andres Burgundy	O	dry
079228	Andres Cabernet Sauvignon	O	dry
086397	Buena Vista Zinfandel	A	dry
027383	Christian Brothers Burgundy	A M O	almost dry
021592	Colony Cabernet Sauvignon	BC A O	faint hint of sugar
026039	Colony Zinfandel	BC A S M	dry
038729	Cribari Cabernet Sauvignon	O	off dry
006239	Gallo Hearty Burgundy	BC A S M O NB NS PEI NFLD	dryish, faintly sweet
020685	Gallo Zinfandel	BC M O Q PEI NFLD	off dry
020941	Inglenook Navalle Ruby Cabernet	BC A Q	dry
038521	Italian Swiss Colony Burgundy	BC A	dry

BOUQUET	TASTE COMMENTS	SUITABLE WITH
fruity	earthy and robust; full deep flavor; a bit harsh but should smooth out with bottle age	braised duck
musty	bitter; thin, no berry flavor	nothing
musty	simple, easy drinking; no complexity; a starter wine	roast veal
burnt edge, smoky	quite dry; almost chalky on palate; bitter overtones	mixed grill
fruity	earthy flavor that lasts; rough and ready	stewed chicken
light, fruity	thin, some fruit; unobtrusive; average	cold cuts
fresh, aromatic herbal	plenty of deep, rough flavor; powerful harsh finish; needs some time to age	lamb curry
faint, woody	light, not much flavor; some bite at first but fades to hot aftertaste	hash browns
forest in spring	powerful and young; very full, almost syrupy; rich and earthy	Stilton
slightly dusty	full earthy flavor; fresh, somewhat harsh but interesting	chili
heady, soft, hint of berries	young and full, needs aging; astringent; pleasant, fruity, herbal flavor	roast beef au jus
powerful, full	ripe and deep flavor, almost stewed; rough but enjoyable	salami sandwiches
heady, plummy	light style; not much depth; grows on you; appealing aftertaste; slightly hot	ham and cheese sandwiches
anticipates berries	thin, not much flavor; flat, somewhat metallic; harsh finish	dull dishes
rich, fruity	bland, chemical taste; going nowhere	chicken livers

RED WINES

REF. NO.	DESCRIPTION	PROVINCES AVAILABLE	RELATIVE SWEETNESS

AMERICAN (continued)

REF. NO.	DESCRIPTION	PROVINCES AVAILABLE	RELATIVE SWEETNESS
078865	Jean Escalle California Red	O	medium sweet
086389	Louis Martini Pinot Noir	A	dry
080010	Parducci Gamay Beaujolais	A	quite dry
017905	Paul Masson Cabernet Sauvignon	A S M O	dry
052308	Paul Masson Gamay Beaujolais	BC	sweetish
008268	Paul Masson Pinot Noir	BC A S M	dry
037275	Sebastiani Zinfandel	A	dry
024067	Sebastiani Mountain Burgundy	BC A S M O	medium dry
075176	Summit Burgundy	O	dry
085035	Sutton Hill California Cabernet Sauvignon	BC	dry

AUSTRALIAN

REF. NO.	DESCRIPTION	PROVINCES AVAILABLE	RELATIVE SWEETNESS
063669	Hardy's Saint Thomas Hermitage	BC A S O	dry
079210	Hardy's Shiraz Cabernet	O	dry
104083	Hill Smith Petit Sirah	O	dry
031971	Kaiser Stuhl Bin 55 Burgundy	BC A	dry
049510	Lindeman's Saint Cora Burgundy	BC A	medium dry

BOUQUET	TASTE COMMENTS	SUITABLE WITH
spicy	quite fruity but almost medicinal flavor; good color	sausages and eggs
burnt, moldy	bitter taste; thin, vegetable flavor	brown rice
fruity	smooth with power and depth; slightly bitter aftertaste	rack of lamb
clean	some depth and complexity; flavorful, balanced	lamb chops
perfumy	flavor of young, unripe berries	calves' liver
light, woody fragrance	flat, light bodied, not much flavor or depth; dull	meatballs
fresh berries	zesty, full bodied, young; lots of bite; grows on you	roast beef
blackberries	thin, tart aftertaste; simple drinking	barbecued spareribs
a bit berry	young, fruity, a bit thin, flat aftertaste but good value	fried chicken
oaky, lovely	very pleasant, full bodied and flavorful; somewhat bitter aftertaste	game
mild, flowery	lots of *oomph*; smooth, clean after-taste	pot roast
full of fruit	medium bodied; flavor of ripe fruit; good length; will last; try aging	barbecued lamb
blackberries	Mother earth in the bottle; big, lots of body; will age very well	*filet Napoleon* or other fine beef dishes
flowery	full bodied, tannic; heavy, earthy flavor that lasts; a bit flat but attractive	barbecued ribs
soft, touch of fruit	smooth but lacks freshness; clean finish; sound plonk	enchiladas

RED WINES

REF. NO.	DESCRIPTION	PROVINCES AVAILABLE	RELATIVE SWEETNESS

AUSTRALIAN (continued)

073692	Mildara Cabernet Sauvignon	O	dry
042465	Yalumba Four Crown Claret	BC O	dry

AUSTRIAN

040592	Blue Danube (Lenz Moser)	BC S M O NFLD	medium dry
043513	Schluck (Lenz Moser)	M O	dryish

BULGARIAN

078881	Gamza (Vinimpex)	BC A O Q NFLD	quite dry

CANADIAN

011635	Andres Auberge	M O NS	medium dry
078246	Andres Botticelli	BC S M O	sweet
080739	Andres Cellar Cask	A S M O NS	medium dry
018408	Andres Dinner	O NB NS	sweet
087957	Andres Domaine D'Or	BC O	dry
087544	Andres Eagle Ridge	BC O	sweet
079251	Andres Fiorino	O	semidry
078907	Andres Lake Country	M O	medium sweet
088682	Andres Pacific Coast Cellars Dry Red	BC A S	medium dry
088351	Andres Red Wine	M O	sweetish

BOUQUET	TASTE COMMENTS	SUITABLE WITH
full, grapey	full bodied, almost chewable; a hearty taste but a bit flat; acceptable	chili con carne
pronounced cherry	refreshing; young and hearty; faint hint of sweetness at first; yummy	wild game birds
light	weak; hint of sweetness; expendable	nothing
light, flowery	light, mild flavor; no zest	grilled cheese
pleasant but faint	fruity; young, good potential; hold for a couple of years	braised beef
foxy; sinus clearing	heavy fruity flavor but slips away; bitter but nice	Irish stew
overripe passion fruit	slightly pétillant, very sweet; alcoholic soda pop	nothing
full, foxy	newly pressed grape juice; sickly sweet	maple sugar, bacon and pancakes
plain, foxy	fresh and pleasant with a bit of personality; a wine for the young	dormitory parties
thin, foul	very pale, almost no flavor; thin, cheap taste	stale bread
rubbery	would rate high as fruit juice; watery cough syrup	cookies after school
foxy	headache material; harsh and thin	acetylsalicylic acid
grapey, smoky	light and sweetish quaffing wine; drinkable; hot finish	adult board games
grapey, earthy	chemical flavor; good to the first drop but not after	no food
grapey	a generic wine	no-name products

RED WINES

REF. NO.	DESCRIPTION	PROVINCES AVAILABLE	RELATIVE SWEETNESS

CANADIAN (continued)

REF. NO.	DESCRIPTION	PROVINCES AVAILABLE	RELATIVE SWEETNESS
011942	Andres Richelieu Cabernet Sauvignon	A	dry
086025	Barnes Heritage Estates Burgundy	O NS NFLD	dry
086041	Barnes Heritage Estates Claret	O	slightly dry
037127	Barnes Ontario Country	O	slightly sweet
078998	Barnes Vin de Table	A S M O	dry
031716	Brights Baco Noir	M O PEI	dry
082743	Brights Dry House Wine	BC S O	dry
075234	Brights Entre-Lacs	S M O NB PEI	dry
015339	Brights House	O	semisweet
020065	Brights Manor Saint Davids Dry	A S M O NB NS	dry
015941	Brights President Burgundy	O	touch of sweetness
081505	Brights Riuscita	O Q	syrupy
061481	Charal Baco Noir	O	dry
081455	Charal Chandelle	O	fairly dry
079236	Charal Chandelle Rouge	O	bittersweet

BOUQUET	TASTE COMMENTS	SUITABLE WITH
light, pleasant	earthy, almost gravelly; like a dry sacramental wine	beef curry
grapey	harsh, tannic; strong taste	ham and cheese sandwiches
full, asters and berries	full bodied; pronounced flavor of overripe cherries; somewhat harsh and warm aftertaste	game
smells sweet	château de screwtop; a tad artificial; tastes like black currants	soda in the afternoon
dry, flowery	fruity with lots of bite; flavor of ripe berries; drinkable	lamb chops
decaying strawberries	smoky; chemical taste, reminds one of an anatomy lab	bread and cheese and cross-country skiing
faintly fruity, pleasant	full bodied, bitter; strong chemical aftertaste	mother-in-law for lunch
rasberryish, simple	harsh artificial berry flavor at first; softens up; drinkable plonk	leftovers
candyish	might be grape powdered-drink mix; lingeringly bad	ice cubes
tinge of fox-iness	lots of pucker-power; hint of *labrusca*	marinating figs
faintly chemical	bitter, some bite; foxy finish	apples
faintly foxy	a communion wine; very sweet; candylike; clings to the mouth	peppermint pie
fruity	zesty with good flavor; light, adequate	bacon and eggs
like grape juice	drinkable; not much personality but goes down easily	bridal showers
strong, floral berrylike	refreshing fruit; soft, some body; pleasing on the palate	lamb chops

RED WINES

REF. NO.	DESCRIPTION	PROVINCES AVAILABLE	RELATIVE SWEETNESS
CANADIAN (continued)			
061838	Charal Maréchal Foch	O	slightly sweet
057166	Charal Premiére Rouge	O	off dry
079244	Château des Charmes Cour Rouge	O	dry
057349	Château des Charmes Gamay Beaujolais	O	dry
064006	Château des Charmes Primeur Rouge	O	dry
049114	Château des Charmes Sentinel Rouge	A O	dry
014712	Château-Gai Cartier Regal Rouge	A O	medium sweet
013136	Château-Gai Cavallo Rosso	A O Q NB NS PEI NFLD	dryish
082206	Château-Gai Chianno Rosso	A S O NB NS	medium dry
011486	Château-Gai Maréchal Foch	O NB	dry
076729	Château-Gai Princiére	O Q NB	dry
004986	Château-Gai Red Medium Dry	A S M O	medium sweet
014993	Château-Gai Regal	O	sweet

BOUQUET	TASTE COMMENTS	SUITABLE WITH
berryish, full	jammy; slightly burnt taste; harsh at first but smooths out; fades quickly	antipasto
full but yeasty	tangy; slightly sweet but lots of bite; soda pop	drive-in horror movies
light, spicy	hard to find a wine taste; thin	soda
very fruity, hint of smoke	light but mouth-filling flavor; tart on the tongue but smooths out and fades quickly	pepper steak
mellow, a bit yeasty	light and pleasant; some taste; decent plonk	pork chops or chicken
mild, pleasant, piquant	harsh initially but smooths out; light, not much zest or taste; tired wine	schnitzels
gaseous	rather like sweet water with a foxy taste; overtones of the Concord grape	popsicles
barely noticeable	innocuous; nondescript	bland food
foxy, fruity	flat, dull and watery; lacks body and flavor; harsh, hot aftertaste	pizza with anchovies
elusive; hint of overripe fruit	light, some fruit; boring but acceptable	veal and cheese dishes
synthetic; sweet soda pop	no taste; watery; unappetizing	tomato juice
woof!—puckers the nose	fresh Concord flavor; more like rosé than red wine; cloying finish	cinnamon as mulled wine
heavy foxy nose	sweet grape juice; jarring old-style *labrusca*; cloying aftertaste	castor oil

RED WINES

REF. NO.	DESCRIPTION	PROVINCES AVAILABLE	RELATIVE SWEETNESS
CANADIAN (continued)			
012039	Château-Gai Seibel	S M O PEI	dry
078956	Colio Rosso	S O	slightly sweet
078964	Colio Rosso Secco	O	cherry pop
088450	Colio Rubino	O	medium sweet
088112	Cuvée des Moins de l'Abbaye (les Entreprises Verdi Inc.)	Q	dry
016832	Géloso Cuvée Rouge	O Q	dry
088336	Grand Patron	O	dry, mellow
082016	Inniskillin Brae Rouge	A S O	medium dry
023341	Inniskillin Chelois	O	dry
075291	Inniskillin de Chaunac	M O	dry
082776	Inniskillin Gamay Noir	O	dry, fruity
011726	Inniskillin Maréchal Foch	O NB PEI	dry
078915	Jordan Grande Cuvée	M O	dry
030718	Jordan Maréchal Foch	O NS	dry

BOUQUET	TASTE COMMENTS	SUITABLE WITH
pungent; rotting leaves	thin; unpleasant flavor that fades; don't swallow!	1000-year-old eggs
slightly spicy	thin but pleasant; drinkable	pork sausages
medicinal	thin; astringent; leaves a coating on the top of your mouth; reminiscent of grape juice	sore throats
full, grapey, Beaujolais-like	a summer red; fizzy but pleasant and refreshing; lots of flavor; acidic; serve chilled	ice and lemon
youthful, fruity	sharp; odd flavor; almost syrupy texture yet short of fruit; harsh aftertaste	corned beef hash
faint, nearly fruity	sharp but good flavor; thin, mild; doesn't last too long	plain food
subdued; slightly yeasty	medium body; simple and straightforward; some fruit but tart; so-so	ham steak
tarry, smoky	a bit harsh; some flavor; reasonably palatable	spicy chicken
fresh, full	some bite; fairly fruity; light, some flavor	summer sandwiches
light, fruity	young but bland; artificial	meatloaf
full, fruity	medium body; fruity but earthy flavor; quite drinkable	barbecued ribs
young, fruity, full	young, fresh taste; an easy drinking wine; Beaujolais-like; somewhat metallic aftertaste	pâté and picnics
faint, toxic	similar to homemade; rough—could use new shock absorbers	go-cart racing
seems off	bites back; thin, little taste; slightly sour aftertaste; short	beef curry

RED WINES

REF. NO.	DESCRIPTION	PROVINCES AVAILABLE	RELATIVE SWEETNESS
CANADIAN (continued)			
019745	Jordan Maria Christina	A S M O NB	sweet
009910	Jordan Toscano	A M O NS NFLD	dryish
070631	L'Entre-Côte (Société des alcools du Québec)	Q	dry
101840	Mission Hill Burgundy	BC	slight hint of sweetness
100040	Mission Ridge Dry Red	BC	dry
020891	Sainte Michelle Zinfandel	BC S	dry
006755	San Gabriel Canadian Burgundy	A	semisweet
082768	Villa Cusato Vino Rosso	O	dry
CHILEAN			
047951	Cabernet Sauvignon (Conch Y Toro)	A M O NS	dry
FRENCH			
031542	Baron de Gardenay (Henri Maire)	Q	dry
074971	Beau Palais (Loron)	O	dry
020776	Beauchoisy (Chapin & Landais)	O Q	dry
054189	Beaujolais Comte de Migieu (Poulet)	O	dry

BOUQUET	TASTE COMMENTS	SUITABLE WITH
peachy smell	tastes a bit like grapefruit; not unpleasant	fraternity parties
neutral	some almond taste; a mild, nothing wine	marzipan
pungent, cheap	harsh in throat; bitter on tongue; looks fruity but actually thin and watery	canned spaghetti
like fermenting apple juice	light, astringent; unpleasant aftertaste; nothing to write home about	turkey à la king
fresh berries	full and young; chewy texture; try aging	flank steak
light raspberry nose	almost a dark rosé; very pleasant fruit taste; quaffable; slightly bitter aftertaste	wieners and beans
very light	pleasant flavor that fades to nothing; mediocre	beach lunches
pleasant	some foxy taste creeps in; wine is full, somewhat tannic and drinkable	spaghetti with spicy sauce
spicy	fruity, young, bites back; good but not special	goulash
caramelization, oxydized nose	artificial tasting; somewhat tannic	instant pudding
fresh, forward, flowery	plenty of fruit and bite; goes down easily; nothing special but good everyday wine	Sloppy Joes
faint mushrooms	dry, crisp, berry flavor; ribbon of sweetness in the middle; tastes good but not great	veal sandwiches
mild fruit	dry and tasty; medium body; spicy; good balance	picnic fare

RED WINES

REF. NO.	DESCRIPTION	PROVINCES AVAILABLE	RELATIVE SWEETNESS
FRENCH (continued)			
027508	Beaujolais la Ribote (Bichot)	BC A O Q	quite dry
037879	Beaujolais Supérieur (Anjou)	BC	dry
009431	Beaujolais Supérieur (Bouchard Aine)	BC A S M Q NB	dry
040311	Beau-Rivage (Borie-Manoux)	A S M O	dry
027920	Belle Amie (Schröder & Schyler)	BC A S M O Q NS PEI NFLD	dry
089938	Bellerive Red (Chauvenet)	O	dry
042879	Bergerac (Unidor)	A	slightly sweet
090829	Bordeaux (Société des alcools du Québec)	Q	dry
035733	Bordeaux Supérieur (Dumons)	O	dry
041087	Burgogne les Ursulines (Cruse)	O Q	dry
079095	Burgogne Passetout-grain (Chauvenet)	O Q	dry
064097	Canteval Rouge (Nicolas)	S M O	dry
070417	Cellermaster (Rodet)	S O NB NS PEI	dry
033530	Château Bellegarde (Borie-Manox)	Q	dry pleasant
037291	Château de Cadillac (Giraud)	S M O Q	dry

BOUQUET	TASTE COMMENTS	SUITABLE WITH
fleeting	good, fruity flavor in the mouth; somewhat harsh; slightly bitter aftertaste	chicken and tarragon
fruit but not much	light, pleasant but innocuous	boiled chicken
earthy, pleasant	thin, watery; no finish; no staying power	light veal dishes
floral, light	thin, light; a bit of fruit; peppery but little sharpness; bitter aftertaste	shish kabob
fresh fruit	light and bland; average sound wine for everyday	meatloaf
light berry nose	soft with some fruit taste; an easy drinking wine; straightforward	roast lamb
nominal	young and fresh; straightforward, light wine; no distinct flavor	beef sandwiches
very slightly fruity	light, some flavor but fruit fades; a little harsh; could soften with age	eggplant casserole
fresh fruit and flowers	a spark of life here; austere; some elegance and depth of flavor; could improve with age	filet with Bordelaise sauce
sinus-clearing	listless; some fruit and body but not notable	liver and onions
perfumy	simple and straightforward; little character; bland	underseasoned burgers
pleasant cedar aroma	medium body and length; plenty of fruity flavor; good plonk	veal chops
light and fruity	earthy, full bodied; not much fruit; rough and ready wine	barbecued spareribs
mild fruit	supple; a bit grassy; medium weight	steak
fruity	pleasant, some acid, long lasting on the palate; good dinner wine	beef tenderloin

RED WINES

REF. NO.	DESCRIPTION	PROVINCES AVAILABLE	RELATIVE SWEETNESS

FRENCH (continued)

REF. NO.	DESCRIPTION	PROVINCES AVAILABLE	RELATIVE SWEETNESS
021626	Château de Douzens Corbiéres (Andrieu Père & Fils)	Q	medium dry
092098	Château du Haut Marquisat (Borie-Manoux)	Q	dry
032474	Château Goumin Bordeaux (Lurton)	Q	medium dry
036012	Château la Grande Chapelle Bord	Q	very dry
088161	Château Saint Germain (Calvet)	O	dry
083626	Corbières (Granier)	O	dry
091207	Corbières (Société des alcools du Québec)	Q	dry
007336	Costières du Gard (Barton & Guestier)	O Q NB NS	dry
032623	Côteaux de Pierrevert (La Blaque)	O	dry
077388	Côtes de Gascognes (Bouchard Aine)	O NB	dry
006643	Côtes du Luberon (Barton & Guestier)	M O Q NB NS	dry
040287	Côtes du Rhône Château Bois de la Garde	Q	dry
079103	Côtes du Rhône (Château la Borie)	BC M O	dry
036566	Côtes du Luberon (Pascalet)	BC	dry

BOUQUET	TASTE COMMENTS	SUITABLE WITH
pungent, grapey	lightweight; no real fruit; bland but a bit thin	hamburger
nonexistent	thin and dry; a minor wine	pasta with canned tomato sauce
insipid	light; short; insufficient fruit	fruit ice cream
woody with jammy finish	very young tasting; lots of alcohol; not very complex; should improve in time	steak
earthy	earthy; long in finish; light; bitter aftertaste; has potential	Dijon lamb chops
faint	light; not much fruit; taste fades quickly; thin and unappealing	ham quiche
closed in; not much	deep and tannic; flavor of young berries there but hiding; some aging should release	moussaka
faint, pleasant	has flavor, body and fruit, but somewhat harsh; good aging potential	barbecued ribs
very slight, satisfactory	light, artificial; alcohol shows through; slight musty tang afterwards	sandwiches in the locker room
musty	light, watery and not much taste; dull	veal Parmesan
missing to faint	tart flavor that lasts; adequate; puckery aftertaste	braised veal shanks
rich, dried raisins	hefty, fruity and tannic; good drinking	strongly flavored dishes
fresh berries	chewy, almost "cooked" taste; good, plain, full bodied effort; earthy flavor and finish	nachos
hopeful, refreshing	a caressing wine; unsophisticated but long and strong	weekday dinners

RED WINES

REF. NO.	DESCRIPTION	PROVINCES AVAILABLE	RELATIVE SWEETNESS

FRENCH (continued)

REF. NO.	DESCRIPTION	PROVINCES AVAILABLE	RELATIVE SWEETNESS
020370	Côtes du Rhône (Domaine de la Tour)	O	dry
014829	Côtes du Rhône (Mommessin)	O Q	dry
091140	Côtes du Rhône (Société des alcools du Québec)	Q	dry
050005	Côtes du Ventoux Beauvillion (Vigna)	O	dry
057497	Crozes Hermitage (Jaboulet)	M O NFLD	dry
017616	Cruse Tradition (Cruse)	O	dry
039941	Cuvée de Robiteau	BC A	dry
081737	Cuvée Jean Calvet (Calvet)	Q	dry
045310	Cuvée Red (Bouchard Aine)	A M	dry
070680	Cuvée Spéciale (Barton & Guestier)	BC O NB NS PEI	dry
092056	Domaine de la Grange (Kressman)	Q	dry
020222	Domaine de la Meynarde (Rhone)	Q	dry
083634	Domaine de Romilhac	O	dry
039719	Domaine de Torraccia (Sichel)	A Q	dry
092254	Domaine Prat-Majou (Société des alcools du Québec)	Q	dry

BOUQUET	TASTE COMMENTS	SUITABLE WITH
fruity, complex	soft and pleasant; quite light; straight-forward quaffing wine	veal stew
faint	straightforward, hale and hearty; easy drinking	barbecued lamb
faint, flowery	smooth, full, slightly burnt finish; good straightforward wine	chopped liver
full, fruity	light and mellow; some real flavor but not special; good *vin ordinaire*	mixed grill
buried fruit	earthy flavor; deep and tannic; good food wine	elegant beef dishes
faint, earthy	like an earthy wine gum but drink-able; hot finish	well-done cheeseburgers
vanilla	light bodied but sharp on palate; pleasant, strong aftertaste	tortellini
slightly artificial	medium bodied; some tannin; uncom-plicated but not much fruit in evidence	hamburgers
nice	full bodied but thins out; sturdy drinking	solid peasant fare
alcoholic	soft and quaffable with some flavor; light, uncomplicated; slightly bitter aftertaste	bangers and mash
black cur-rant but tinny end	tannic, harsh; little fruit; quite astringent	beef stew
fruity	soft, well balanced; long finish; a little bitterness in the end	pizza
fruity	harsh at first but rounds out; fruity medium body and full aftertaste	lamb stew
sulphury	artificial; tasting of candies	spicy sausage
sulphuric	light bodied, close to a rosé in style; a quaffing wine at best	patio meals

RED WINES

REF. NO.	DESCRIPTION	PROVINCES AVAILABLE	RELATIVE SWEETNESS
FRENCH (continued)			
091520	Don Quixote (Société des alcools du Québec)	Q	dry
032565	Fitou (Union Des Caves Haut.)	Q	dry
093427	Gamay de Touraine (Wine Guild)	S M	dry
074995	Grand Chartrons (Johnston)	O	dry
021980	Grand Seigneur (Poulet)	O Q	dry
055061	La Cour Pavillon (Loudenne)	BC A S M O Q NS NFLD	dry
032086	La Fleur du Roy (Schröder & Schyler)	Q	dry
035477	Le Berger Baron Rothschild (P. de Rothschild)	BC S Q	dry
039909	Le Gamain Red (Hasenklever)	O	dry
033829	Le Grilladon (Malesan)	O Q	dry
072744	Le Piat D'Or (Piat)	S M O NB NFLD	not too dry
074997	L'Epayrie (Roux)	O NB NS NFLD	dry
085969	Les Chais (Loudenne)	S O NS	dry

BOUQUET	TASTE COMMENTS	SUITABLE WITH
aromatic, slightly burnt	light but flavorless; could be grape-flavored alcohol	soya burgers
fruity, elegant, burnt oak	fruit sustained in mouth; young; some complexity	roast meats
off-geranium	some fruit and flavor, not bad, but can't get past the smell	fried garlic
faint sandal-wood	austere; fruit closed in—could use some bottle age; pleasant, medium body	steak sandwich for lunch
almost none	not bad; a bit thin; better as it mellows; smooth going down; not much flavor	chips
pleasant	medium body; tasty, good balance; good food wine	roast lamb
grassy	very supple; easy drinking; a little faint	chicken
lovely, some fruit	light bodied; fruity and smooth; some bite; slightly bitter aftertaste	*coq au Bordelaise*
fruity but disappears quickly	good fruit and well balanced; layered flavors; very drinkable	*filet Napoleon*
subdued, some fruit	medium body; straightforward *vin ordinaire* with some bite; not distinctive	roast chicken
soft	full bodied; well balanced; very drinkable; smooth	chicken
faint	inoffensive but decent plonk; some fruit; all-purpose table wine	hearty chicken dishes
toasted almonds	reminiscent of fruit and nuts; young and astringent; straightforward	submarine sandwiches

RED WINES

REF. NO.	DESCRIPTION	PROVINCES AVAILABLE	RELATIVE SWEETNESS

FRENCH (continued)

REF. NO.	DESCRIPTION	PROVINCES AVAILABLE	RELATIVE SWEETNESS
005314	Lion Rouge (Calvet)	BC A M O	dry
091082	Mâcon N.V. (Société des alcools du Québec)	Q	dry
041350	Mâcon Supérieur (Bouchard Père et Fils)	BC O	dry
023226	Medoc (Cruse)	A	dry
035337	Medoc (P. de Rothschild)	BC A	dry
082727	Minervois (Chantovent)	BC O	dry
028449	Minervois Château de Beaufort (Schröder & Schyler)	O	very dry
022384	Minervois Château de Courgazaud	Q	dry
044040	Minervois Prieure Madeleine (Hasenklever)	O	dry
000513	Mommessin Export (Mommessin)	BC A S M O Q NB NS NFLD	dry
079079	Moreau Rouge (Moreau)	O Q	rather dry
000943	Mouton-Cadet (P. de Rothschild)	BC A S M O Q NB NS PEI NFLD	dry
074989	Père Patriarche (Patriarche)	BC M O Q	dry
002618	Prince Noir (Barton & Guestier)	BC A S M O Q NB NS NFLD	dry

BOUQUET	TASTE COMMENTS	SUITABLE WITH
small, very light; disappears	light, thin, not enough fruit; ordinary	lunch
no bouquet	tart; uninteresting; astringent	cheese slices
sweetish, grapey	lean with some sweetness; tart finish; pleasant taste but alcohol shows through	walnuts
black currants	a little tannin; thin; bouquet is the best part	ham steak
musty	thin and harsh; sharp finish	baked beans
full, fruity	heady; some bite and fruit at the beginning; good, easy drinking without much character	barbecued hot dogs
light fruit, agreeable	forward, fruity taste; some bite; good balance; fruit stays with you; pleasant aftertaste	filet mignon
grapy; forthcoming nose	supple; fruity; not complex but honest quaffing wine	pizza
slight	typical, sound, inexpensive wine; no special qualities; pretty good	steak sandwiches
light, dusty	light style but drinkable; thin and unexciting	linguine
dusty, warm nose	acidic with some fruit; goes down easily; commercial	flank steak
light, musty nose	straightforward light wine; not much zip; vin ordinaire	potato skins
bay leaf	some flavor but fades quickly; tart at first but improves	barbecued chicken wings
clean, fresh	dry, hint of bitterness; light with some fruit flavor; clean, smooth finish; good plonk	leftover lamb

RED WINES

REF. NO.	DESCRIPTION	PROVINCES AVAILABLE	RELATIVE SWEETNESS

FRENCH (continued)

014225	Prix Rouge	BC O NB	dry
002493	Réserve des Moins (Bichot)	BC O Q NB PEI	dry
039990	Réserve du Château (Cruse)	A	off dry
003715	Sélection (Kressman)	BC A S M O Q NB NS PEI NFLD	dry
039099	Tourne Broche (Calvet)	Q	dry
049668	Vins de Pays Coteaux de Baro	Q	medium dry
099515	Vin de Table (Lichine)	O	dry

GREEK

078873	Apelia Courtakis	BC M O	dry
085522	Apollo Courtakis	O	dry

HUNGARIAN

007203	Egri Bikavar (Monimpex)	BC A S M O Q NB NS NFLD	dry
000794	Szekszardi (Monimpex)	BC A S M O Q NB NS PEI NFLD	dry

ISRAELI

021501	Carmel Cabernet Sauvignon	M O Q	dry

ITALIAN

038174	Barbera (Fontanafredda)	A M O	dry

BOUQUET	TASTE COMMENTS	SUITABLE WITH
warm, inviting	light style, nondescript, but sound; a wine for all seasons	dinner with friends
soft, flowery	young and quite palatable; has a nice texture	*tortière*
faint hint of grape	tart on the tongue; light and not much taste; bitter finish	desperation dinners
pleasant, fruity	round and smooth but forgettable; a computerized blend; a wine for all purposes	Silicon Valley Parties
not much	straightforward, well balanced; fresh; good value	flank steak
roasted oak	it attacks you at first sip; fruity but some acid around edges	barbecued shish kabob
faint	some flavor but thin and watery; blah	canned ham
weak, some fruit, hint of yeast	sharp, some flavor but doesn't last long	a cheap date
lightly fruity	fruity, tannic; somewhat medicinal—maybe it's good for you; good but peculiar	dancing on the beach
sweet, fruity	fruity taste; somewhat bitter but quite drinkable	haggis
weak, chemical aroma	insipid; light and flat; passable taste; bitter aftertaste	2-day-old sandwiches
light, her-baceous	some taste; touch of acid on finish; young and puckery; stays with you	duck
complex, licorice	full, tannic, long finish; plenty of flavor	game pie

RED WINES

REF. NO.	DESCRIPTION	PROVINCES AVAILABLE	RELATIVE SWEETNESS
ITALIAN (continued)			
0485385	Barbera del Monferrato (Bersano)	A	dry
026369	Barbera del Piemonte (Kiola)	S O Q	dry
033613	Barbera, Villa Doria	BC	dry
072868	Bardolino Classico	M	dry
012344	Bardolino (Folinari)	S M O	dry
045443	Bardolino (Negrar)	A O	dry
020214	Barolo (Fontanafredda)	BC A O Q	dry
024992	Cabernet (Or. Fe. Vi.)	O	dry
078899	Cabernet Franc (Valdo Aquilea)	O	dry
026849	Cantinello (Vinitalia)	O	quite dry
010579	Castelli Romani (Co. Pro. Vi.)	O	dry
001016	Castelli Romani (Colli Albani)	BC M O NS PEI NFLD	dry but not sharp
085977	Caveneto Cabernet (La Gioiosa)	O	dry
012773	Chianti (Bertolli)	O Q	dry
005017	Chianti (Melini)	A S M O Q NB NS PEI	dry
001743	Chianti (Ruffino)	BC A S M O Q NB NS PEI NFLD	dry

BOUQUET	TASTE COMMENTS	SUITABLE WITH
light, musty	full bodied, mild and pleasant; good company wine	barbecued steaks
burnt flowers	thin, watery; some flavor and fruit but dull	a warm fire
light, tempting	harsh, tannic; needs more aging and less additives	salami sandwiches
frail	bitter; could pass as wine vinegar	salad dressings
off—sour milk	very light; harsh but smooths out; lacks quality; barely drinkable	ham and eggs
geraniums	chemical taste; bland; thin; ordinary	cola drinks
medium; complex	beautiful garnet color; full depth of flavor; long, tasty finish	steak or game
faint, musty	light but flavorful; some bite; smooth and delicious	lamb
clears the nose	tannic, musty; light but bitter; mediocre	garlic sausages
fabricated; black currant jello	sour, pasteurized flavor; bitter on the palate; not pleasant	boxed macaroni dinner
slightly fruity	light and fairly pleasing; not much *oomph!*	steak sandwich for lunch
full, some fruit	pleasant; fruity and well balanced but dull; won't offend	dinner with your in-laws
jammy fruit	dull but no flavor; not offensive; mediocre	cioppino
dank-cellar nose	smooth but dull; light and tasty but taste fades; competent, everyday staple	lasagna
off—tooth-paste?	thin; alcohol comes through before the grape; plenty of bite but a bit metallic; adequate	Sichuan beef
earthy, robust	smooth, drinkable, some fruit and tannin; promising, try aging	candlelight dinners in 1986

RED WINES

REF. NO.	DESCRIPTION	PROVINCES AVAILABLE	RELATIVE SWEETNESS
ITALIAN (continued)			
091322	Chianti (Société des alcools du Québec)	Q	dry
003962	Chianti Classico (Brolio)	BC A S M O Q NS NFLD	dry
075093	Chianti Classico (Melini)	BC O	dry
045195	Chianti Classico Riserva Ducale (Ruffino)	BC O Q NB	dry but fruity
068247	Colli Berici (Zonin)	O	dry
034439	Corvo Rosso	O	dry
003046	Donini Vino di Verona (Lamberti)	BC A S M O Q NS PEI NFLD	dry
075028	Giacondi (Cierrevi)	S M O NB NS PEI NFLD	dry with hint of sweetness
026062	Merlot (Casarsa)	O Q	dry, not tart
013342	Merlot (Collavini)	BC A O Q	dry
079186	Merlot del Piave (Or. Fe. Vi.)	O	hint of sweetness
028423	Montepulciano d'Abruzzo	O	dry
078816	Pinot Nero (Ponte)	O	dry
080713	Prego (S.A.B.R.I.)	O	off dry

BOUQUET	TASTE COMMENTS	SUITABLE WITH
faintly pungent	very light; short of fruit; dull; flavor fades quickly	grapes
herbal	fruity with some flesh; good taste and length; hint of almonds in aftertaste	veal chops
light	tart; astringent but some real flavor; a sound food wine	sauerbrauten
soft, fruity, intense	soft fruit flavor; some bite; medium body; good balance; impressive	veal dishes
fresh and fruity	very pleasant flavor; livens the mouth gently; medium bodied; tasty, good for quaffing	nibblies in the jacuzzi
nil	tart; sharp taste that stings; some flavor; a zingy wine	lamb curry
thin, almost nonexistent	very pale; lacks fruit and flavor; high in acid; unacceptable	anything alkaline
fruity but harsh	fruity and straightforward; somewhat bland and lacks bite; O.K. but just O.K.	undiscerning palates
faint, fruity, pleasant	light and fruity; tart but good balance; good plonk, easy drinking	chicken in cream sauce
roasted almonds	pleasant; some fruit but not much; alcohol dominates	gorgonzola
ripe cherries	pleasing, fresh taste; chewy cherrylike flavor; full and round; slightly tart	a hearty family dinner
faint	powerful and full; almost chewable; flavor lasts and lasts	lamb goulash
weak, fruity	light and inoffensive; wishy-washy; bitter aftertaste	beer nuts
fresh, slightly fruity	light with some bite; harshly flowery; pleasant enough but not much character	pasta at your favorite trattoria

RED WINES

REF. NO.	DESCRIPTION	PROVINCES AVAILABLE	RELATIVE SWEETNESS
ITALIAN (continued)			
053884	Refosco (Casarsa)	O	dry
078824	Riviera del Garda (Premiovini)	O	dry
014951	Rosso d'Abruzzo (Tallo)	O	dry
082610	Rossofiore (Umberto)	O	dry
041947	Rubesco (Lungarotti)	BC A O	dry
064386	Sangiovese di Romagna (Cellini)	BC	dry
079194	Solopaca (Rosso)	O	dry
089334	Spanna (Umberto Fiore)	O	dry
000828	Valpolicella (Folonari)	BC S M O Q	dry
019307	Valpolicella (Lamberti)	A O Q NS	dry
008334	Valpolicella (Negrar)	A M O	dry
012443	Valpolicella Valpantena (Bertani)	O Q NS	dry
091389	Valpolicella (Société des alcools du Québec)	Q	dry
082222	Villa Ambra (Fabiano)	O	dry
060996	Vino Nobile di Montepulciano	M	dry

BOUQUET	TASTE COMMENTS	SUITABLE WITH
a bit of fruit	tart but drinkable—some flavor	Chinese sausage
simple, fruity	young and tough but fruity; tannic as leather bootlaces; should mellow with age	black pudding
slightly fruity	smooth and hearty; good everyday wine	beef stew
fresh and raunchy	very fruity; rough and ready flavor that fades; raw and unsubtle	garlic chicken
warm, complex	full of flavor, depth and complexity; a great buy	red meat with strong sauces
neutral	young, fruity, lots of bite; a tongue tingler	garlic spareribs
smooth	tart, some depth; a little short on flavor but plenty of *oomph;* young but not likely to age	pork shoulder roast
full, fruity	hint of sweetness on tongue; some bite and depth of flavor; needs time	lamb stew
weak, peppery	too tannic; leaves a distinct aftertaste of something you'd prefer to forget	nightmares
mild	bland; some fruit but thin and light; not much substance	ham omelet
faint	has a bite; sharp aftertaste but good flavor; drinkable	Italian sausages
whiff of fruit	straightforward with some class and power; finishes well; fruit drying out, drink now	carpaccio
yeasty	thin and bland; some flavor of fruit which turns sour on the finish	licorice candy
fresh bread	zesty flavor, like fresh raspberries; round and gaining subtlety; plenty of body	tacos
flowery	peppery, hearty, strong; a hot wine	spicy Italian food

RED WINES

REF. NO.	DESCRIPTION	PROVINCES AVAILABLE	RELATIVE SWEETNESS

PORTUGUESE

038646	Alianca	O	parched
014977	Dao (Grao Vasca)	A S M O Q NB NFLD	dry
010892	Dao Terras Altas (Fonseca)	BC A M O Q	dry

SOUTH AFRICAN

009704	Bonne Esperance	BC M O NFLD	dry
062950	Fleur du Cap	A O	dry
022004	Paarl Cabernet Sauvignon	BC M O PEI NFLD	dry
023978	Paarl Pinotage	O	dry
007187	Paarl Roodeberg	BC A S M O NB NS PEI NFLD	dry with hint of sweetness

SPANISH

041574	Carta de Plata (Barberana)	O	dry
029728	Coronas (Torres)	BC O Q	dry
091439	Feu Follet (Société des alcools du Québec)	Q NB NFLD	dry
079657	Lancorta (Landalan)	O	dry
039776	Montelorca	A S M O	some sweetness
011577	Oleya (Dubonnet)	M O NB	dry

BOUQUET	TASTE COMMENTS	SUITABLE WITH
a bit of fruit	fruity but a little harsh; mouth puckering; thin	vinegary sauces
fruity	flavorful but acidic; full bodied	raucous barbecue
woody	medium body; earthy flavor, a bit short on the finish	pork pie
chemical aroma	light, somewhat rough; a students' wine	studying
faint	plenty of flavor; somewhat bitter, warm finish	pork roast
herbaceous	full, medium flavor; good body; astringent; fruit is buried	chili con carne
assertive, fruity	a bit hard at first but softens up; nicely balanced; yummy; stays with you	pork cassoulet
aromatic, smoky	full bodied; smooth with some bite; not much depth; everyday all-purpose wine	corned beef hash
full	young, good potential; has some complexity; lay down for a couple of years	roast beef
mild, woody	medium body, fruity taste; smooth finish; not bad but a long way from great	beef casserole
fruity, full	light style; tart on the tongue; grapy flavor but not enough of it	barbecued shrimp
full, grapey	powerful yet soft; slightly musty; enjoyable	lamb stew
alcoholic	thin, woody; heavy aftertaste	pretzels
soft, fruity	fruity, homemade flavor, somewhat flat	bistro food

RED WINES

REF. NO.	DESCRIPTION	PROVINCES AVAILABLE	RELATIVE SWEETNESS
SPANISH (continued)			
080028	Rocamar (Amigo)	M O Q	dry
006585	Sangre de Toro (Torres)	BC A S M O Q NS PEI	dry
075184	Senorio de Ulia	O	moderately dry
004960	Siglo (Age)	A M	dry
072793	Vina Santa Digna (Torres)	M	dry
YUGOSLAVIAN			
017608	Kastelet (Dalmacijavino)	O Q	dry
030239	Merlot (Slovin)	A S M O	dry

BOUQUET	TASTE COMMENTS	SUITABLE WITH
hoplike	pleasant quaffing wine; tart aftertaste; good value	beef stew
delicate	full bodied; harsh at first blush but smooths out; pleasant	chili con carne
currant jam	very light, drinkable style; hint of vanilla but not much fruit	mild cheeses
fruity	amazingly together for a young wine; quite gentle	paella
harsh	acidic; strong aftertaste	curried lamb
prickly	astringent but some fruit; thin; bitter but likable; nice afterbite	sweet and sour pork
fuzzy, musty smell	light and soft; fruit fading, not much bite; drying out, sagging	old lace

ROSÉS

REF. NO.	DESCRIPTION	PROVINCES AVAILABLE	RELATIVE SWEETNESS
AMERICAN			
06899	Paul Masson Rosé	A	sweet
CANADIAN			
028613	Andres Auberge	M O	dryish
111408	Andres Dinner Rosé	O NS	sweet
86140	Barnes Heritage Rosé	O	medium dry
015339	Brights House Rosé	M O NB PEI	semisweet but dryish
081455	Charal Chandelle	O	fairly dry
024398	Château-Gai	O NFLD	medium sweet
081448	Château-Gai Gamay Rosé	O NB	dry
013318	Château-Gai Pink	BC S M O	dry
14993	Château-Gai Regal	O	sweet
082594	Colio Rosato	O	sweet
017947	Inniskillin Rosé	O	almost dry
FRENCH			
100115	Mommesin Rosé	O	dry
012641	Rosé d'Anjou (Remy-Pannier)	BC A S M O Q NS	medium dry
081661	Royal de Neuville Anjou Rosé	S M O	sweet

BOUQUET	TASTE COMMENTS	SUITABLE WITH
clean, fruity	grape flavor but flat; weak; tastes like a lo-cal wine	fruit punches
fruity	uninteresting but quite sippable; serve very chilled	afternoon tippling
plain, foxy	fresh and pleasant; has a bit of personality; soda pop	19th birthday parties
none that's discernible	a little tart; deceptive, tastes very alcoholic but drinkable	strawberries
candyish	might be grape powdered-drink mix; lingeringly bad	ice cubes
like grape juice	drinkable; not much personality but goes down easily	bridal showers
negligible	some grape taste; cloying aftertaste	not much
fishy	flat and pungent; clears the sinuses; odd taste	sardines
chemical smell	amber colored; dreadful	sour milk
heavy foxy nose	sweet grape juice; jarring old-style *labrusca*; cloying aftertaste	castor oil
light and fruity	spicy with a real bite; not delicate but not bad	poolside
foxy, fruity	foxy taste; light, almost watery	fried egg sandwiches
heady	dry tasting, powerful but fleeting	red snapper Provençale
metallic	like homemade crabapple wine; burns halfway down	pork chops
nutty	flat, has some resemblance to wine; stemmy or bitter underneath sweetness	a threat

ROSÉS

REF. NO.	DESCRIPTION	PROVINCES AVAILABLE	RELATIVE SWEETNESS

PORTUGUESE

006854	Casal Mendes Rosé	BC A S M O Q NB PEI NFLD	medium sweet
018861	Faisca Rosé Fonseca	BC A S M NFLD	sweet
000166	Mateus Rosé (Sogrape)	BC A S M O Q NB NS PEI NFLD	medium sweet

SPANISH

| 110114 | Marquis de Cacères | O | dry |

BOUQUET	TASTE COMMENTS	SUITABLE WITH
light	slightly fruity; pleasant but flat	boating parties
slight	sweet touch of fruit; metallic undertones	fruit salad
flowery	zippy, fruity taste; well balanced but suburban	your first dinner party
alcoholic	soft, fruity, powerful enough for meats	strongly flavored foods

SPARKLING WINES

REF. NO.	DESCRIPTION	PROVINCES AVAILABLE	RELATIVE SWEETNESS
CANADIAN			
083417	Andres Asti Bianco	A S M NB NS	sweet as soda pop
003814	Andres Baby Champagne	BC A S M O NB NFLD	moderate
000091	Andres Baby Duck	BC A S M O Q NB NS PEI NFLD	very sweet
003319	Andres Chante Blanc	BC A S M O Q NS PEI NFLD	sweet
101402	Andres Cordoba Blanca	O	off dry
016659	Andres Richelieu	M O Q	sweetish
083170	Andres Spumante Christallo	A S M O NS PEI NFLD	medium sweet
033431	Barnes Grand Celebration	M O	very sweet
028803	Barnes Spumante Bianco	M O NS NFLD	medium sweet
001230	Brights President Dry	BC S M O Q NB NFLD	medium sweet
009183	Brights President Pink	BC M O	sweet
089375	Château-Gai Alpenweiss Spar	BC A O NS	medium sweet
013201	Château-Gai Imperial Dry	BC A S M O NB NS PEI NFLD	fairly sweet
033209	Château-Gai Imperial Brut	BC A S M O Q NB NS PEI NFLD	sweetish
83287	Cusato Spumante	O	very sweet
001826	Jordan Spumante Bambino White	BC A S M O NS PEI NFLD	very sweet

BOUQUET	TASTE COMMENTS	SUITABLE WITH
reminiscent of raisins	initially fruity but no finish; a sparkling wine for unsophisticated palates	a bowling banquet
light	could this be soda?; attractive but not much life	a Sunday afternoon movie
muscat	cream soda or cherry pop	popsicles
muscat	pleasant muscat flavor; light and fresh but sweetness stays with you	the late show
slight	nice mousse; tastes a bit thin but pleasant; drinkable	scallop mousse
seltzer	light and watery	soda water
faint rosé, unobtrusive	bland; mousse fades quickly; tart	hash
faint, pleasant	smooth bubbles; plenty of flavor but very sweet; like sweet soda pop	office celebrations
pungent	not much taste; like a grapy cream soda; cloying on finish	soap operas
assaults the nose, foxy	tastes like candy apples; strong *labrusca* aftertaste	Halloween
grapey	too many bubbles—hides the taste which is just as well	marinating strawberries
pungent, muscat aroma	good balance of flavor and sweetness; pleasant, crisp	wild strawberries and whipped cream
small and unpleasant	frothy; foxy, artificial apple flavor; not quite awful	poaching apples
flat	mellow with some bite; bubbles fade out; not everyone's cup of champagne	teen toasts
pleasant	good color and mousse; very sweet, spumantelike; flavor like ice cream	zabaglione
light	unctuous, tastes like soda pop	chips, pretzels

SPARKLING WINES

REF. NO.	DESCRIPTION	PROVINCES AVAILABLE	RELATIVE SWEETNESS
FRENCH			
042267	Frederic Chopin (Wissembourg)	M O	off dry
006742	Greyman Brut (Berger)	M O Q NS	medium sweet
GERMAN			
003491	Henkell Trocken	BC A S M O Q NB NS PEI NFLD	medium dry
053637	Konzert (Scholl & Hildebrand)	O PEI NFLD	semisweet
030825	Kupferberg Gold	A	medium sweet
093963	Schloss Prinz Franz Reh	O	sweet
ITALIAN			
29520	Gran Sante (Tombolini)	O	sweet
SPANISH			
000968	Codorniu Gran Cremant	BC S M O Q NB NFLD	off dry
078774	Codorniu Extra	BC A O Q	dry
099507	Conde de Caralt	O	dryish
078782	Dom Yago (Santyago)	O	a bit sweet
074757	Freixenet Carta Nevada	BC M O NB PEI	lemony sweet
088591	Freixenet Cordon Negro	BC O Q	dry

BOUQUET	TASTE COMMENTS	SUITABLE WITH
fruity with hint of yeast	light, crisp and fresh; quite palatable; light mousse	a good party
weak but flowery	light and inoffensive; fading bubbles; bland	pretzels
light, fruity	fresh, a bit lemony; light and pleasant	cassis as cocktail
closed in	easy drinking but dull; bubbles alive	orange juice
fresh	no finish but some flavor	marinating strawberries
appley	harsh, overlaid by flimsy veil of fruit	elderly aunts
geraniums	tastes like ginger ale with lemon	pizza
nutty, earthy	not much flavor but a pleasant warm finish; satisfactory	smoked salmon mousse
spicy, a bit yeasty	large bubbles; earthy flavor with bitter finish; good drinking	birthday toasts
yeasty lemon	good flavor; tart and lemony; pleasant dry style	strawberries
1953 Chevy hubcaps	harsh, thin and somewhat flat; overtones of ginger ale; some fruit and taste	oysters
smoky, earthy	tastes smoky with almond overtones; subdued	oysters
faint, smoky	interesting and different taste; bubbles fade; slightly bitter aftertaste	nibbles on paper plates

BEST BUYS

The highest rated white and red wines have been classed as "Super Buys" and are listed first. These wines represent the best value at the liquor store regardless of price. The other wines listed here—also very good buys—are subdivided into three categories: 1) Canadian wines, 2) wines under $6.00, and 3) wines over $6.00.

NOTE: Not all wines listed in all provinces.

WHITE WINES

Super buys
005405   Badacsonyi Szurkebarat (Monimpex)
010884   Blanc de Blancs (Calvet)
036582   Cuvée les Amours (Hugel)
040972   Graves (N. Vernaux)
083238   Kremser Schmidt (Krems)
063628   Pinot Bianco (Fontanafredda)

Canadian
001719   Brights House
011247   Brights President Extra Dry
081596   Charal Chandelle Blanc
056754   Château des Charmes Chardonnay
081562   Château des Charmes Nokara Riesling
080604   Château-Gai Chardonnay
079780   Inniskillin Vidal
010686   Jordan Toscano
101774   Mission Hill Chenin Blanc
023267   Rêve d'été (Société des alcools du Québec)
082818   Villa Cusato

Under $6.00
036913   Alsace Coquillages (Trimbach)
046821   Donini Vino di Verona (Lamberti)
041285   Entre-Deux-Mers (P. Bouchard)
079020   Frascati Superiore (Marino)
028340   Liebfraumilch Rheinkeller
040683   Lindeman's Ben Ean Moselle
093393   Lindeman's White Burgundy
027698   Orvieto Classico (Melini)
006833   Paarl Riesling
083774   Raimat Can Casal (Coniusa)
045229   Traminac (Navip)
082230   Villa Ambra (Fabiano)

099549   Vin de France (Lichine)
062745   Zeller Grafschaft (Kurfurstliche)

Over $6.00
073783   Bereich Wonnegau Erben Spätlese (Langguth)
073254   Côtes du Rhône (Mommessin)
018432   Liebfraumilch Crown of Crowns
040741   Monbazillac (S.I.C.A.)
018002   Moselmaid (Deinhard)
047399   Paul Masson Chenin Blanc
029918   Roc Blanc (Cruse)
038018   Rudesheimer Rosengarten (Kendermann)
075697   Summit Chablis
050161   Vouvray Chenin Blanc
029157   Wiltinger Scharzberg Zentral

RED WINES

Super buys
064097   Canteval Rouge (Nicolas)
003962   Chianti Classico (Brolio)
057497   Crozes Hermitage (Jaboulet)
104083   Hill Smith Petit Sirah (Hill Smith)
072744   Le Piat D'Or (Piat)
041947   Rubesco (Lungarotti)

Canadian
061838   Charal Maréchal Foch
064006   Château des Charmes Primeur Rouge
023341   Inniskillin Chelois
011726   Inniskillin Maréchal Foch
100040   Mission Ridge Dry Red
020891   Sainte-Michelle Zinfandel

Under $6.00
054189   Beaujolais Comte de Migieu
089938   Bellerive Red (F. Chauvenet)

041574	Carta de Plata (Barberana)
001016	Castelli Romani (Colli Albani)
001743	Chianti (Ruffino)
036566	Côtes du Luberon (Pascalet)
091140	Côtes du Rhône (Société des alcools du Québec)
020370	Côtes du Rhône (Domaine de la Tour)
045310	Cuvée Red (Bouchard Aine)
078881	Gamza Vinimpex
039909	Le Gamain Red (Hasenklever)
079657	Lancorta (Landalan)
049510	Lindeman's Saint Cora Burgundy
022384	Minervois Château Courgazaud
044040	Minervois Prieure Madeleine (Hasenklever)
079079	Moreau Rouge (Moreau)
017905	Paul Masson Cabernet Sauvignon
014951	Rosso d'Abruzzo (Tallo)
089334	Spanna (Umberto Fiore)
075176	Summit Burgundy
085035	Sutton Hill California Cabernet
039099	Tourne Broche (Calvet)
082222	Villa Ambra (Fabiano)
042465	Yalumba Four Crown Claret

Over $6.00

038174	Barbera (Fontanafredda)
020214	Barola (Fontanafredda)
088161	Château Saint Germain (Calvet)
040287	Côtes du Rhône Château de la Garde
045195	Chianti Classico Riserva Ducale (Ruffino)
079103	Côtes du Rhône (Château la Borie)
014829	Côtes du Rhône (Mommessin)
079210	Hardy's Shiraz Cabernet
055061	La Cour Pavillon (Loudenne)

ROSÉS

110114	Marquis de Cacères

SPARKLING WINES

Under $6.00
089375   Château-Gai Alpenweiss

Over $6.00
078774   Codorniu Extra
099507   Conde de Caralt
042267   Frederic Chopin (Wissembourg)
003491   Henkell Trocken

PART TWO
THE
FOOD

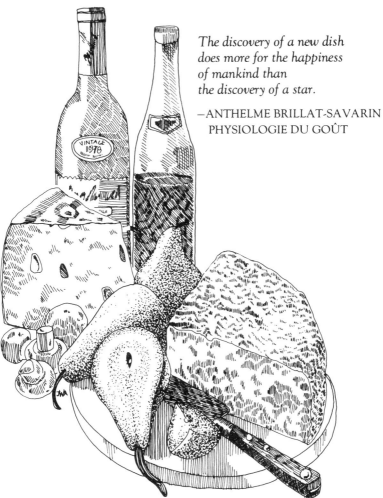

*The discovery of a new dish
does more for the happiness
of mankind than
the discovery of a star.*

—ANTHELME BRILLAT-SAVARIN
PHYSIOLOGIE DU GOÛT

INTRODUCTION

A wine guide without food is like summer without sun. Wine by itself can be savored, appreciated and enjoyed, but in conjunction with food it reaches new heights.

The food section which follows consists of sixteen menus for different occasions ranging from a sensational brunch to an after-theater indulgence. I have suggested appropriate wines for each menu, but use your own knowledge and experiment widely.

There are tips on giving a wine tasting party, recipes, wine punches, suggestions for using leftover wine, and a treatise on cheese.

Here is a simple guide for matching food with suitable wines.

Soup   If white wine is served with the meal, serve it with the soup. If red wine is offered, pour it after the soup. Sherry is often served with soup.

Fish   The common rule is white wine with fish and shellfish. White Burgundies, Bordeaux, Hocks, and Moselles are especially fine. If you cook fish in a red wine, that wine should accompany the dish.

Poultry   Both white wine and the lighter reds go well with poultry. Duck and goose call for more powerful reds.

Meat   Serve red wine with red meats, the flavors complement each other.

Salad   Wine is never drunk with salad because the vinegar in the dressing cuts the wine taste.

Dessert   Serve the rich, sweeter wines with dessert— Sauternes or German sweet wines, for example.

BACK TO BASICS

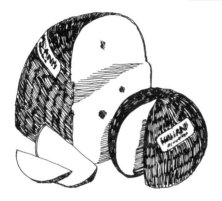

Here are some explanatory notes and basic recipes to help ensure success in the menus that follow.

Baking blind   Place wax or foil paper on pastry. Weight down with beans or rice. This prevents pastry from puffing up during baking.

Bouquet garni   Don't bother with muslin bags—use a bay leaf, two stalks of parsley, and a stalk of thyme if you can get them. Tie them together with string or use a tea egg to hold the herbs.

Butter   Use unsalted butter in all recipes.

Glazing tarts   Use red jelly for red fruits and apricot jam or apple jelly for yellow fruits.

Herbs   If you have fresh herbs use three times the quantity of dried ones.

Lining a flan pan   Roll pastry around a rolling pin. Ease
    into flan pan. Press down gently. Roll pin across top of
    ring to remove excess pastry.

Mushrooms   They should be wiped, not washed, because
    they retain water.

Peeling tomatoes   When tomatoes are used in a dish they
    will look more attractive if the skins are removed.
    Simply immerse the tomatoes in boiling water for 30
    seconds, then plunge into cold water. The skins will
    slip off easily.

Poaching   To poach means to cook foods very gently in
    water or other liquids at a temperature below a
    simmer.

Reducing sauces   Many sauces in this book are made by
    reducing wine, stock, and cream. When you use this
    method each ingredient should be reduced before the
    next one is added to thicken the sauce. Use whipping
    cream as other creams do not have as high a butterfat
    content and will curdle if boiled.

To refresh   Pour cold water over drained, cooked vegeta-
    bles to stop further cooking. For rice, refresh with hot
    water to remove some of the starch.

Unmolding   Place the mold in hot water for ten seconds.
    Put a plate on top. Always dampen the plate first.
    Then if your mold isn't perfectly centered, you can
    slide it easily into position. Reverse the plate and
    voilà!—a beautiful mold. If the sides run a little, mop
    up the spills with a paper towel.

Vinaigrette   If your vinaigrette is too oily add salt to cut
    the oiliness.

BASIC RECIPES

These recipes appear in both imperial and metric measures.
Metric measures are not always equivalent to imperial. In

some cases numbers are rounded up or down to make it simpler to follow the recipes, and none of the flavor is lost.

STOCK

Stock is not soup so don't look for a full, hearty flavor. Stock is used in conjunction with other ingredients to produce soups and sauces. You can make your own or use canned beef or chicken broth. In a pinch use good quality stock cubes, but remember if you reduce them the resulting sauce will be too salty. All stock freezes well. By storing it in your freezer in two-cup containers or plastic bags you will always know the exact quantity you are defrosting.

Stock keeps in the refrigerator about a week as long as it is strained; in the freezer about six months.

BEEF STOCK

When making stock you don't have to worry about exact measurements. Approximate quantities will not spoil it.

4 lb	beef bones	2	kg
2 lb	veal knuckles	1	kg
2 lb	short ribs	1	kg
4	carrots, in chunks	4	
4	onions, in chunks	4	
2	stalks celery	2	
6	mushroom stems	6	
1	tomato, sliced, or ends of tomatoes	1	
8	peppercorns	8	
	water to cover bones		

Brown bones in 450 F (230 C) oven until a good dark color, about 30 minutes. Pour off fat and transfer all ingredients to stock pot. Cover with water to 1-inch (2.5 cm) above bones. Bring to a boil. Skim off the scum as it rises slowly to the surface. Simmer until reduced by half, about 4–8 hours.

CHICKEN STOCK

3 lb	chicken backs and necks or bones	1.5 kg	
1	large onion, in chunks		1
1	large carrot, in chunks		1
1	stalk celery		1
	green onion tops, if available		
	leek tops, if available		
6	peppercorns	6–8	
	bouquet garni		

Place all ingredients in stock pot. Cover with water 1-inch (2.5 cm) above the contents. Bring to a boil. Skim off foam as it rises. Simmer slowly until reduced by one-third. Strain, refrigerate, and skim off fat when stock is needed.

FISH STOCK

3 lb	fish bones and heads	1.5 kg	
1	onion, in chunks	1	
1	carrot, in chunks	1	
	pieces of leek		
½ cup	dry white wine	125 mL	
	bouquet garni		
6–8	peppercorns		

Place all ingredients in stock pot. Cover with water to 1-inch (2½ cm) above the bones and simmer no longer than 1 hour. The stock will turn bitter if cooked longer.

CRÈME FRAÎCHE

A slightly soured cream which thickens naturally without whipping. It can be used with tarts or in sauces as a substitute for thick cream.

1	cup	whipping cream	250 mL
⅓	cup	sour cream	75 mL

Mix with a wire whisk. Let sit in a warm place for 12 hours. Refrigerate for 24 hours before using. It will be thick.

MENUS
AND
RECIPES

Champagne is for breakfast.

—GEORGE BAIN

A TENSION-FREE BRUNCH

Leek and Egg Gratin

Savory Tart

Celeriac Salad

Pavlova with Kiwi Fruit

Recommended wines
Blanc de Blanc (Calvet)
Château-Gai Sparkling Alpenweiss
Colio Bianco Secco

to serve eight

To be a relaxed and refreshed hostess and avoid getting up at 6 a.m. to cook, this brunch is ideal. Although it can be prepared the day before, it will look and taste as fresh and as delicious as if it had been assembled at the very last minute.

Leek and Egg Gratin

The secret of this dish is to scramble the eggs very lightly and let them finish cooking while in the oven. Any cooked vegetable can be substituted for the leeks.

6	tbsp	butter	75 mL
1	bunch	leeks, washed and thinly sliced	1 bunch
1	cup	whipping cream	250 mL
12		eggs	12
		salt and pepper	
¼	cup	whipping cream, extra	50 mL
½	cup	grated Gruyère cheese	125 mL
½	cup	grated Parmesan cheese	125 mL

Melt 4 tablespoons (50 mL) butter in a frying pan,

add the leeks, and coat with the butter. Cover and cook over low heat until limp, about 10 minutes. Turn heat to high, add 1 cup (250 mL) cream, and boil the sauce down until thick.

Beat 10 of the eggs in a large bowl. Beat the remaining 2 eggs in a small bowl. Melt the remaining butter and gently scramble the 10 eggs, whisking all the time. While still moist, remove from heat and beat in the extra 2 eggs. Season with salt and pepper and cool.

Preheat oven to 400 F (200 C).

In a 4-cup (1 L) buttered gratin dish, layer half the scrambled eggs, the leeks, then the remaining scrambled eggs. Sprinkle with the extra cream. Cover with the grated cheeses. Bake until browned on top, about 15 minutes.

Savory Tart

This tart can be cut into small slices and served cold as an hors d'oeuvre.

Pastry

3	cups	all-purpose flour	750	mL
1½	tsp	salt	7	mL
1	cup	butter	250	mL
2		cloves garlic, minced	2	
4	tbsp	water	75	mL
4	tbsp	dry white wine	50	mL

Filling

2	lb	fresh spinach	1	kg
		grated nutmeg		
1	lb	mushrooms, sliced	500	g
12	tbsp	butter	175	mL
		juice of ½ lemon		
3		leeks, washed and sliced, or 1 Spanish onion, sliced	3	
2	tsp	thyme	10	mL

8 oz	crab meat	250 g
3	eggs	3
1½ cups	whipping cream	375 mL
	salt and pepper	
½ lb	Gruyère cheese,	
	grated	250 g

Preheat oven to 425 F (220 C).

Pastry by food processor method: Process the flour, salt, butter, and garlic together. With the machine running, add liquids. Transfer contents of bowl to a work surface and gather into a ball.

Pastry by hand method: Cut the butter into the flour. Add the garlic and salt. Sprinkle with the liquids and gather into a ball.

Roll out the pastry to fit into a rectangular baking dish 12 × 8-inches (30 cm × 20 cm) or a 12-inch (30 cm) flan pan. Cover the pastry with foil and weight it with dried beans. Bake 15 minutes.

Filling

Wash the spinach and steam until wilted. Drain well. Squeeze out all liquid and chop coarsely. Sprinkle with nutmeg. Reserve.

Over high heat, sauté the mushrooms in half the butter until soft. Moisten with lemon juice. Reserve. Sauté the leeks in remaining butter until soft. Sprinkle with thyme. Reserve.

Drain the crab meat. Combine the eggs and cream.

To assemble: Preheat oven to 375 F (190 C). Layer spinach, crab meat, mushrooms, and leeks, seasoning each layer with salt, pepper, and a sprinkling of cheese. Pour the egg/cream mixture over the top, using a fork to encourage the liquid to penetrate the layers. Top with remaining cheese and bake for 30–35 minutes.

Variation: Omit the crab meat.

Celeriac Salad

Celeriac is also known as celery root. It is not the root of the more familiar celery plant, but its cousin. The taste is similar to celery. Celeriac leaves are not eaten.

2	lb	celeriac	1	kg

Dressing

1½	cups	mayonnaise	375	mL
3	tbsp	Dijon mustard	50	mL
4	tbsp	finely chopped parsley	50	mL
2	tsp	tarragon	10	mL
4	tbsp	white wine	50	mL
4	tbsp	lemon juice	50	mL

Peel the celeriac and cut it into thin strips. If using a food processor cut with the shredder blade. Combine all ingredients for the dressing. If the consistency is too thick, thin out with a little hot water.

Toss the dressing with the celeriac. Serve on a flat dish, mounding the salad in the center.

Pavlova with Kiwi Fruit

Pavlova is a dessert named after the famous Russian ballet dancer, Anna Pavlova. It is as light and ethereal as her dancing is reputed to have been. This particular version uses kiwi fruit as the garnish, but any other attractive fruit may be used.

4		egg whites	4	
3	tbsp	water	50	mL
1	cup	sugar	250	ml
1	tbsp	white vinegar	15	mL
1	tbsp	cornstarch	15	mL
1	tsp	vanilla extract	5	mL
		pinch of salt		

½ tsp	cream of tartar	2 mL
1 cup	whipping cream	250 mL
3	kiwi fruit, peeled and sliced	3

Preheat oven to 275 F (140 C).

Line a cookie sheet with parchment paper.

Beat the egg whites until stiff. Add the water and beat again. Gradually add the sugar, beating well after each addition. Add the vinegar, cornstarch, vanilla, salt, and cream of tartar. Beat the mixture with an electric mixer until thick and glossy.

Mound onto the cookie sheet in an 8 × 10-inch (20 cm × 25 cm) circle.

Bake 1 hour without opening the oven. Cool and remove from paper.

Whip the cream until soft peaks form. Cover the ring with the softly whipped cream. Decorate with kiwi fruit slices.

On the day before: Prepare the leek and egg gratin. Refrigerate until 1 hour before baking.

The savory tart can be baked, refrigerated, and reheated when needed. Celeriac salad tastes better if it marinates overnight. The Pavlova meringue can be baked and stored in an airtight container until needed.

On the day: Bake the leek and egg gratin just before serving.

Whip the cream for the Pavlova and decorate it with kiwi fruit. It can stand for a couple of hours without problems.

A SIMPLE FALL LUNCH

Zucchini and Mushroom Frittata

Tomato, Watercress, and Orange Salad

Crème Brûlée

Recommended wines
Frascati Superiore (Marino)
Jordan Selected Riesling
Sainte Michelle Chenin Blanc

to serve six

This is a light lunch and not too filling.

Zucchini and Mushroom Frittata

A frittata is a kind of flat omelet made in a frying pan and can be large enough to serve up to six people. The vegetables for the fillings can be varied depending on what is in season.

8	tbsp	butter	125	mL
1		clove garlic	1	
2		small zucchini, thinly sliced	2	
		salt and pepper		
1		leek, washed and finely chopped	1	
6	oz	mushrooms	200	g
1	tbsp	fresh basil or	15	mL
1	tsp	dried	5	mL
1	tbsp	lemon juice	15	mL
12		eggs	12	
½	cup	whipping cream	125	mL

½ cup	grated Gruyère cheese	125 mL
3 tbsp	chopped parsley or	50 mL
	chives	

Over high heat, melt 3 tablespoons (50 mL) of the butter, add the garlic, and immediately toss in the zucchini slices. Sauté until limp, seasoning well with salt and pepper.

Remove zucchini from the pan. Add another 3 tablespoons (50 mL) of butter. Sauté the leek for 1 minute, then add the mushrooms. Sprinkle with basil and sauté until the mushrooms begin to lose their liquid. Moisten with lemon juice. Season with salt and pepper.

Remove from heat and combine with the zucchini.

Preheat broiler.

Beat the eggs with the cream and add to zucchini and mushroom mixture.

In a 12-inch (30 cm) frying pan, melt the remaining 4 tablespoons (100 mL) of butter over medium-high heat. When the butter sizzles, pour in the egg and vegetable mixture and shake the pan slightly. Cook for about 3 minutes, or until set at the bottom. Sprinkle with the cheese and place the pan under the broiler until the top is golden and the mixture has set.

Cool for 1 minute. Loosen the sides with a spatula and flip frittata onto a serving plate. Garnish with chopped parsley or chives and serve immediately.

Tomato, Watercress, and Orange salad

Very refreshing and beautiful to look at.

Dressing

9 tbsp	olive oil	150 mL
3 tbsp	wine vinegar	50 mL
1 tbsp	sugar	15 mL
1 tbsp	lemon juice	15 mL
	salt and pepper	

Salad

2	oranges	2
4	tomatoes, thinly sliced	4
1	head Boston lettuce	1
1	red onion, finely chopped	1
1 tbsp	chopped parsley	15 mL
1	bunch watercress, cleaned and trimmed	1

Combine all dressing ingredients and beat well. Reserve.

Peel the oranges, removing all the white pith. Cut into circles. On a flat platter, alternate orange and tomato slices on a bed of lettuce. Sprinkle with the onions and parsley. Pour the dressing over and garnish salad with watercress.

Crème Brûlée

This custard dessert was first served to the students of Trinity College, Cambridge, where it soon became a favorite.

2 cups	half-and-half or whipping cream	500 mL
4	egg yolks	4
¼ cup	sugar	50 mL
½ cup	sugar for caramel	125 mL

Bring the cream to a simmer. Beat the egg yolks and ¼ cup (50 mL) sugar together until well combined. Add the warm cream. Transfer mixture to a heavy pot or double boiler.

Over low heat, stir the mixture until slightly thickened. Pour into a 4-cup (1 L) gratin dish and cool. Sift the sugar for caramel evenly over the top. Place under a broiler and watch carefully until the sugar has caramelized. Chill and serve.

On the day before: Prepare the crème brûlée and refrigerate until needed. Peel and slice the oranges, leave in their own juice, and refrigerate. Prepare and sauté the vegetables for the frittata and refrigerate.

On the day: Assemble salad in the morning. Make the fritatta just before serving.

A FASHIONABLE WINTER DINNER

Scallops with Saffron and Pernod

Filet Napoleon with Bordelaise Sauce

Sautéed Vegetables

Frozen Orange Mousse with Chocolate Sauce

Recommended wines

first course

Entre-Deux-Mers (Paul Bouchard)

Graves (Cruse)

main course

Hill Smith Petit Sirah

Le Gamin (Hasenklever)

to serve eight

This dinner is designed for impressive entertaining. A lot of steps are required, although none are particularly difficult.

Scallops with Saffron and Pernod

This is a dish that tastes as spectacular as it looks.

2 cups	fish or chicken stock	500	mL
½ cup	dry white wine	125	mL
1 tsp	saffron	5	mL
1½ lb	scallops or shrimp	750	g
1 tsp	Pernod, or to taste	5	mL
1 cup	whipping cream or	250	mL
	Crème Fraîche		
	(see p 121)		
	Parsley sprigs		

Simmer the stock, wine, and saffron for 5 minutes. Add the scallops and poach for 3–4 minutes, depending on size of scallops. Remove and keep warm. Over high heat, reduce the sauce by half. Add the cream, but do not stir. Reduce again until the sauce lightly coats a spoon. Add the Pernod and stir to blend. Spoon the sauce over the scallops. Serve on individual plates. Garnish each with a sprig of parsley.

Filet Napoleon with Bordelaise Sauce

This simple and elegant dish is an updated version of Beef Wellington. The meat is roasted, sliced, and then laid on pastry rectangles covered with duxelles. Because it is not encased in pastry, slicing problems are eliminated and you can gauge beforehand how your beef will turn out.

The thickness of the meat determines the cooking time. Ten minutes to the inch (4 min to the cm) is a good rule of thumb for rare; 15 minutes (6 min to the cm) for medium.

Marinade

1	tbsp	oil	15	mL
1	tbsp	Dijon mustard	15	mL
1	tbsp	brandy	15	mL
		Salt and pepper		
3	lb	beef filet	1.5	kg

Duxelles

1	tbsp	oil	15	mL
2	tbsp	butter	25	mL
2		shallots or green onions, finely chopped	2	
1	lb	mushrooms, finely chopped	500	g
½	cup	whipping cream	125	g
2	tbsp	chopped parsley	25	mL
		salt and pepper		

Pastry

1	lb	frozen puff pastry	500	g
1		egg	1	
1	tsp	salt	5	mL

Bordelaise Sauce

3	tbsp	oil	50	mL
¼	cup	chopped onions	50	mL
¼	cup	chopped carrots	50	mL
¼	cup	chopped celery	50	mL
2	tbsp	all-purpose flour	25	mL
4	cups	beef stock or bouillon	1	L
1	tsp	tomato paste	5	mL
2		mushroom stems	2	
		Bouquet garni (3 parsley stems, 2 springs thyme, 1 bay leaf)		
3		shallots, finely chopped	3	
½	cup	dry red wine	125	mL
2	tbsp	beef marrow	25	mL

To Marinate: Combine all marinade ingredients. Smear over the fillet and leave for 2 hours.

Duxelles

Heat the oil and butter. Add the shallots, stir for 1 minute, then toss in the mushrooms. Cook over high heat until all the mushroom liquid disappears. Add the cream and reduce until cream disappears. Add the parsley and salt and pepper to taste. Let cool and reserve.

Preheat oven to 425 F (220 C).

Roast the fillet for 35–45 minutes depending on how you like to serve it. Remove from oven and let sit for 10 minutes.

To assemble: Roll out pastry into 2 rectangles, approximately 8 × 10-inches (20 cm × 25 cm). Cut each rectangle into 8 pieces. Combine egg and salt for glaze. Place pastry on a damp cookie sheet. Brush with egg glaze. Bake at 425 F (220 C) for 7–10 minutes, or until golden brown.

Arrange 8 pastry pieces on individual serving plates. Reheat mushroom mixture and spread on pastry. Carve fillet into thin slices. Overlap on top of duxelles. Top with the other 8 pieces of pastry. Serve the Bordelaise sauce separately.

Bordelaise Sauce

Heat the oil. Add the vegetables and cook slowly until they begin to brown.

Off the heat, add the flour and stir until well blended. Continue cooking until mixture has nicely browned and has a nutty fragrance.

Off the heat, add the stock, tomato paste, mushroom stems, and bouquet garni. Simmer for 45 minutes and strain.

In another pot, simmer the shallots and red wine until reduced by half. Stir into the sauce together with the beef marrow. Simmer gently for 5 minutes and serve with the beef.

Sautéed Vegetables

Any vegetable in season may be used, but remember to include some green to liven up the appearance of the dish.

1	lb	white turnips	500	g
1	lb	carrots	500	g
3		stalks celery	3	
6	tbsp	butter	100	mL
2	tbsp	chicken stock	25	mL
		salt and pepper		

Julienne the vegetables in a food processor or by hand. Heat the butter and sauté the vegetables for 1 minute.

Lower the heat, add the stock, cover, and cook for 5 minutes. Season well and serve.

Frozen Orange Mousse with Hot Chocolate Sauce

This dessert can be made in a loaf pan, then unmolded and sliced. It can also be served in hallowed-out oranges.

Mousse

¼ cup	water	50 mL
½ cup	sugar	125 mL
8	egg yolks	8
¾ cup	Grand Marnier, Cointreau, or Triple Sec	175 mL
3 cups	whipping cream	750 mL

Hot Chocolate Sauce

1 cup	water	250 mL
½ cup	sugar	125 mL
6 oz	semisweet chocolate	175 g

Mousse

Boil water and sugar together until the syrup reaches the thread stage, 225 F (112 C) on a candy thermometer. To test, dip a wooden spoon into the syrup. When ready, it will drip off the spoon in threads.

Beat the egg yolks with an electric mixer until very thick, then quickly pour in the hot syrup. Beat the mixture until it is thick and mousselike, then beat in the liqueur. Reserve.

Whip the cream until it holds its shape but is not stiff. Fold into mousse.

Spoon the mousse into a 9 × 5 × 3-inch (23 × 13 × 8 cm) loaf pan or 12-inch (30 cm) cake pan lined with plastic wrap. Cover and place in the freezer overnight. Remove 30 minutes before serving. Unmold and slice.

Hot Chocolate Sauce

Boil water and sugar together for 2 minutes. In a separate pot, melt the chocolate over the lowest heat, stirring occasionally. When chocolate has melted, pour in the sugar syrup and stir. Raise heat and simmer until mixture heavily coats a spoon.

Pour the hot chocolate sauce on individual serving plates and place a slice of orange mousse on top. Serve immediately.

On the day before: Bake puff pastry rectangles then refrigerate. They can be reheated when needed.

Prepare the duxelles and refrigerate. Prepare the orange mousse and freeze. Prepare the chocolate sauce and reheat at serving time.

On the day: Marinate the filet.

Cut the vegetables into julienne. They can be sautéed and then reheated, covered, in a moderate oven for 10 minutes.

Roast the filet; it can stand in a foil tent for about 30 minutes.

Prepare the scallops while the filet is roasting.

A THANK-GOODNESS-IT'S SPRING DINNER

Marinated Salmon

Dijon Lamb Chops

Whipped Parsnips

Sautéed Cucumber with Green Onions

Rhubarb and Yogurt Pie

Recommended wines
main course
Barnes Vin de Table
Château Saint Germain (Calvet)
La Cour Pavillon (Loudenne)
dessert
Bereich Wonnegau Erben Spätlese (Langguth)
Orvieto Classico (Melini)

to serve six

This dinner restores the spirit after the winter blues because it features the first food signs of spring.

Marinated Salmon

The raw salmon will "cook" in the lime juice and will even change color in the process. *Sichuan* peppercorns are fragrant in taste, not hot.

1 lb	salmon (tail end)	500	g
	juice of 6 limes or 3 lemons		
1 tsp	coriander seeds	5	mL
12	*Sichuan* peppercorns (optional)	12	
1 tbsp	shallots or finely chopped green onion, white part only	15	mL

2 tsp	tarragon	10 mL
4	green onion tops, finely chopped	4
4 tbsp	olive oil	50 mL
8	firm mushrooms, thinly sliced	8
2 oz	lumpfish caviar	50 g

Slice the salmon thinly against the grain. Place on a platter and pour over half the lime juice. Turn the slices every 30 minutes, four times in all, using the remainder of the lime juice if needed. The fish should turn a light pink. Make sure each piece is thoroughly marinated.

Crush the coriander seeds and peppercorns together. For maximum flavor they should be coarsely cracked. Sprinkle salmon with shallots, crushed seeds, tarragon, green onion tops, and the olive oil. Distribute the salmon slices on 8 plates. Arrange the sliced mushrooms in a flower pattern in the center of each dish. Top mushrooms with tiny heaps of caviar. Refrigerate until needed.

Dijon Lamb Chops

The meat cooks very evenly and retains all its juices.

12	1½–2-inch (4–5 cm) thick lamb chops	12
1	lemon, cut in half	1
	salt and pepper	
6 tbsp	Dijon mustard	100 mL
⅓ cup	finely chopped fresh parsley	75 mL
2	cloves garlic, minced	2
1 cup	bread crumbs	250 mL

Preheat oven to 500 F (250 C).

Rub chops with lemon on both sides, then sprinkle with salt and pepper.

Combine mustard, parsley, and garlic and mix well.

Cover both sides of the lamb chops with equal amounts of the mustard mixture, then coat with bread crumbs.

Place on a rack in a baking pan and bake for 3 minutes. Turn off heat and leave chops in the oven for 30 minutes. They will continue baking until done to pink perfection. If you prefer them medium, leave in the oven another 10 minutes.

Whipped Parsnips

This dish is a good substitute for mashed potatoes. For a taste change, add a dash of curry powder.

2 lb	parsnips	1	kg
8 tbsp	butter	125	mL
	salt and pepper		
	pinch of grated		
	nutmeg		
½ cup	whipping cream	125	mL

Peel parsnips and steam or boil until tender. Purée in a food processor or put through a food mill. Whisk in butter, seasoning, and cream. Transfer to a gratin dish and serve immediately or keep warm in a low oven until needed. This dish reheats well.

Sautéed Cucumber with Green Onions

Cooked cucumber is an unusual dish and quite delicious.

1	English cucumber, peeled	1	
2 tbsp	butter	25	mL
12	whole green onions, white part only	12	
	salt and pepper		
	chopped fresh mint		

Cut the cucumber lengthwise into 4 pieces, then

into 2-inch (5 cm) chunks. Melt the butter in a frying pan and add the cucumber and green onions. Season with salt and pepper. Cover and cook gently for 10 minutes, shaking the pan occasionally. Remove from heat and sprinkle with mint.

Rhubarb and Yogurt Pie

I consider this one of the best pies in the world!

Pastry

1½	cups	all-purpose flour	375	mL
1	tbsp	sugar	15	mL
½	tsp	salt	2	mL
8	tbsp	butter	125	mL
1	tbsp	white vinegar	15	mL
3	tbsp	cold water	50	mL

Filling

1½	cups	sugar	375	mL
⅓	cup	all-purpose flour	75	mL
1	cup	plain yogurt	250	mL
4–4½	cups	diced rhubarb	1	L

Crumble

½	cup	firmly packed dark brown sugar	125	mL
½	cup	all-purpose flour	125	mL
¼	cup	butter	50	mL

Pastry

In a medium-sized mixing bowl, sift together flour, sugar, and salt. Cut the butter into the flour mixture until it resembles coarse meal. Combine vinegar and water and add as much as is needed to form a ball.

Roll out pastry to fit a 9-inch (23 cm) flan pan with removable rim. Roll pastry around rolling pin and transfer to the pan, gently easing pastry into it. Trim off surplus.

Preheat oven to 450 F (230 C).

Filling

Mix the sugar, flour, and yogurt. Combine with the diced rhubarb and spoon into pie shell.

Crumble

Mix together brown sugar and flour. Cut in the butter until the mixture has a crumbly texture. Sprinkle on top of the pie.

Bake for 15 minutes, reduce heat to 350 F (180 C), and continue baking for another 30 minutes. Remove the pie from the pan. Serve hot or cold.

Variation: Add 2 cups (500 mL) of sliced strawberries to the rhubarb before pouring over the yogurt mixture.

On the day before: Prepare the rhubarb and yogurt pie and refrigerate.

On the day: Coat the lamb chops ahead of time. Cook the parsnips; they can be reheated at 375 F (190 C) until hot. Sauté the cucumber and onions. Reheat when needed. Arrange the salmon on serving plates.

AN ELEGANT BUT EASY DINNER PARTY

Cream of Broccoli Soup

Salmon in Phyllo Pastry with Herb Sauce

Green Beans

Chocolate Ruffle

Recommended wines:
Château des Charmes Chardonnay
Kremser Schmidt
Vin de France (Lichine)

to serve eight

This dinner takes a little time to prepare, but the final results are spectacular.

Cream of Broccoli Soup

4	tbsp	butter	50 mL
3		leeks washed, trimmed, and sliced	3
2		potatoes, peeled and cubed	2
3	cups	broccoli flowerets	750 mL
6	cups	chicken stock	1.5 L
1	cup	whipping cream	250 mL
		Salt and pepper	
6	tbsp	chopped chives	100 mL
8	tbsp	grated Parmesan cheese	125 mL

Melt the butter in a large saucepan and sauté the leeks until limp. Add potatoes and sauté for 2 minutes.

Add broccoli flowerets and stock. Bring to a boil and simmer for 20–30 minutes, or until the broccoli is tender. Purée in a food processor or blender.

Add the cream, bring to a boil, and simmer 5 minutes. Season well. Garnish with chopped chives and Parmesan cheese.

Salmon in Phyllo Pastry with Herb Sauce

A splendid dish with a mixture of subtle flavors to enhance the salmon.

2–2½	lb	salmon fileted	1	kg
8	tbsp	butter, softened	125	mL
3	tbsp	raisins	50	mL
3	pieces	stem ginger in syrup, finely choppcd	3	
4	tbsp	coarsely chopped macadamia nuts	50	mL
		salt and pepper		
1	lb	package phyllo pastry	500	g
½	cup	butter, melted	125	mL

Herb Sauce

2	tbsp	finely chopped fresh dill	25	mL
2	tbsp	chopped parsley	25	mL
2		shallots, chopped	2	
2	tbsp	butter	25	mL
2	cups	fish stock	500	mL
1	tsp	Dijon mustard	5	mL
1	cup	whipping cream	250	mL
		lemon juice		
		salt and pepper		
1 each	tbsp	butter mixed with flour	15 each	mL

If possible buy 2 tail pieces of salmon already filleted, or cut the salmon into 2 equal pieces. Combine butter, raisins, ginger, and nuts. Season with salt and pepper. Use the mixture to sandwich the fillets together.

Preheat over to 425 F (220 C).

On a buttered cookie sheet, layer 6 sheets of phyllo pastry, brushing each layer with melted butter before adding the next. Refrigerate pastry for another use.

Place the salmon on top and fold the layers over envelope style so that the fish is completely enclosed. Brush the package with more butter.

Bake for 10 minutes, then turn heat down to 350 F (180 C) and bake for another 20 minutes.

Remove from oven. Slice and serve with herb sauce.

Herb Sauce

Slowly cook dill, parsley, and shallots in butter until limp. Stir in the stock and Dijon mustard. Bring to a boil, then simmer for 10 minutes, or until reduced by half. Add cream and reduce for 1 minute. Add lemon juice, salt, and pepper to taste. Return to a boil and beat in butter and flour mixture to thicken the sauce slightly. Simmer for 2 minutes. Serve with the salmon.

Note: If the salmon piece is too large to be enclosed by the phyllo pastry, overlap 2 sheets to make a larger surface. Butter each double sheet before adding the next.

Green Beans

1½ lb	green beans	750 g
	salt and pepper	
	lime juice	

Bring enough water to cover the beans to a boil. Add green beans and cook until crisp-tender, 3–4 minutes. Refresh with cold water, drain, and season with salt, pepper, and a little lime juice.

Chocolate Ruffle

12 oz	bittersweet chocolate	375 g
½ cup	water	125 mL
⅓ cup	butter	75 mL

½ cup		crushed praline (recipe follows)	125	mL
		rum or brandy to taste		
2 cups		whipping cream	500	mL

Praline

3 oz		almonds, with skin	75	g
1 cup		sugar	250	mL

Break up the chocolate in a heavy pot and add the water. Melt over gentle heat, stirring occasionally until chocolate is thick and creamy. Cool a little.

Cream the butter with an electric mixer. Stir in chocolate and gradually beat in the praline. Flavor with rum or brandy. Lightly oil a 4-cup (1 L) stainless steel bowl or mold. Partially whip 1 cup (250 mL) of the cream and fold it into the chocolate mixture. Transfer to the bowl or mold and refrigerate overnight. Turn out onto serving platter by dipping the mold quickly into hot water. Whip the remaining cream until stiff and pipe a ruffle of cream around the base of the chocolate mold.

To make praline: Put almonds and sugar in a heavy pan. Set on low heat until sugar melts. When it turns a pale gold, stir, and continue cooking until it is nut brown. Pour the praline onto a cookie sheet. Leave until hardened.

Remove from cookie sheet and crush into a coarse powder in a food processor or blender.

On the day before: Prepare the soup and refrigerate. Prepare the salmon in phyllo pastry and refrigerate. Make the chocolate ruffle and refrigerate.

On the day: Prepare the herb sauce. Reheat when needed. Remove salmon from the refrigerator and bring to room temperature before baking. Unmold the chocolate ruffle and pipe with whipped cream. Cook the green beans.

A FAMILY DINNER

Mushroom and Green Onion Soup

Chicken in a Pot

Cabbage with Juniper Berries and Garlic

Strawberry Tart

Recommended wines
Brights House White
Carmel French Columbard
Château-Gai Pinot Chardonnay

to serve six

This dinner is ideal to cook for your family without spending too much time in the kitchen.

Mushroom and Green Onion Soup

When served hot, it tastes like mushroom soup—cold, it resembles an elegant vichysoisse.

8	tbsp	butter	125	mL
25		green onions, including all but 2-inches (5 cm) of the green tops, finely chopped	25	
5	cups	chicken stock	1.25	L
½	lb	firm mushrooms, thinly sliced	250	g
½	cup	whipping cream salt and pepper to taste	125	mL

Garnish

| 6 | firm mushrooms, thinly sliced | 6 |
| ¼ cup | sour cream cayenne pepper | 50 mL |

In a large pot, melt the butter over high heat. When the butter sizzles toss in the green onions and sauté for 1 minute, or until they are coated with butter. Lower the heat, cover, and gently simmer for 10 minutes. The onions should stew without turning brown.

Add the chicken stock and bring to a boil. Simmer for 10 minutes uncovered. Add the mushrooms and simmer for another minute. Remove from heat.

Purée the soup in a food processor or blender. Return to the pot. Add the cream and simmer for another 5 minutes. Taste, adding salt and pepper as needed.

Just before serving, garnish with sliced mushrooms, topping each bowl with a dollop of sour cream and a sprinkling of cayenne pepper.

Chicken in a Pot

This simple and wholesome dish has a sauce thickened with the vegetables that are cooked with it.

3 tbsp	butter	50 mL
1 4–5 lb	chicken	2 kg
1	medium onion, thinly sliced	1
1	carrot, thinly sliced	1
1	thin slice orange with rind	1
1 tbsp	tarragon salt and pepper	15 mL
1½ cups	chicken stock	375 mL
½ cup	whipping cream, optional	125 mL

Orange rounds, rind
and pith removed
(optional)

Preheat over to 400 F (200 C).

Melt the butter in an ovenproof casserole. Brown the chicken slowly on all sides with breast side down. Remove the chicken from the casserole and add onion, carrot, orange slice, and half the tarragon. Cook for 1 minute. Return the chicken to the casserole and sprinkle with salt, pepper, and remaining tarragon. Cover and bake for 1 hour and 15 minutes, basting occasionally.

Remove chicken and set aside. Transfer onion, carrot, and orange slice to a food processor or blender, together with any accumulated juices. Blend well. Add enough chicken stock to make a pouring sauce. Reheat in the original pot and add the cream, if you wish.

Cut up chicken and pour sauce over it. Garnish with orange rounds, if you wish.

Cabbage with Juniper Berries and Garlic

If you don't have juniper berries, add 1 tablespoon (15 mL) of gin before baking.

2	cloves garlic	2	
10	juniper berries	10	
4 tbsp	olive oil	50	mL
1	small cabbage, shredded	1	

Preheat oven to 350 F (180 C).

Mash together garlic and juniper berries.

In a large frying pan, heat the oil and sauté garlic/berry mixture for 30 seconds.

Add the cabbage and toss to coat with oil. Transfer the contents of the pan to a gratin dish and bake 10 minutes. Serve with the chicken.

Strawberry Tart

The chocolate coating on the pastry provides an attractive contrast to the strawberries.

Pastry

1½	cups	all-purpose flour	375	mL
¼	cup	sugar	50	mL
		Pinch of salt		
12	tbsp	butter, cut in small pieces	175	mL
2-3	tbsp	cold water	30-45	mL

Filling

2	oz	semisweet chocolate, melted	60	g
1	quart	strawberries, hulled	1	L

Glaze

1	cup	red current jelly	250	mL

Preheat oven to 425 F (220 C).

Pastry

Sift together the flour, salt, and sugar. Cut in butter until mixture is crumbly. Bind with water, then chill the pastry for 30 minutes. Roll out and press into a 9-inch (23 cm) flan pan. Cover with foil and weight down with dried beans. Bake blind for 15 minutes.

Filling

Remove foil and beans. Return to oven for 5 minutes, or until the pastry is a pale gold.

Cool and brush on melted chocolate, covering bottom and sides. Arrange strawberries in the pastry shell in concentric circles.

Glaze

Heat red currant jelly. Brush onto strawberries, making sure all the spaces are filled to give a better finish.

Variation: To make a more elaborate tart, top chocolate-coated pastry with custard before adding the strawberries.

On the day before: Prepare the soup and refrigerate. Prepare pastry for the tart and bake.

On the day: Fill and glaze the tart, but do not re-frigerate because the glaze will absorb the moisture from your refrigerator and begin to run.

Sauté the cabbage ahead of time and bake just before needed.

This chicken dish does not reheat well; therefore, it should be cooked just before serving.

AN ORIENTAL BANQUET

Bean Curd Soup with Greens

Steamed Fish in Black Bean Sauce

Lemon Chicken

Family Style Beef

Ginger Ice Cream

Recommended wines
Badacsonyi Szurkebarat (Monimpex)
Charal Chandelle Blanc
Inniskillin Vidal

to serve six

If you wish to entertain your friends in a different fashion, here are a few tips on Chinese cooking. Always cut meat and vegetables the same size and shape so that they will cook evenly. Use a wok over the highest heat to ensure food will cook quickly. Deep fry in very hot oil to prevent greasy food. Use a Japanese or Chinese soy sauce.

Bean Curd Soup with Greens

Bean curd firms as it cooks.

6	cups	chicken broth	1.5 L
2		squares bean curd, diced	2
8	oz	any Chinese cabbage or spinach, thinly sliced	250 g
		Soy sauce to taste	
2	slices	ginger, smashed	2 slices
2		green onions, chopped	2

In a large saucepan, combine broth, bean curd, cabbage, soy sauce, and ginger. Simmer for 10 minutes. Remove ginger. Adjust seasoning. Garnish soup with green onions.

Steamed Fish in Black Bean Sauce

You can tell when the fish is cooked by checking the eye. If it has glazed, the fish is ready. Serve the head to the honored guest!

1½–2	lb	firm fish, such as pickerel, snapper, or bass	1	kg
½	tsp	salt	2	mL
1½–2	tbsp	fermented black beans	25	mL
1	clove	garlic, minced	1	
2		thin slices ginger, minced	2	
2		green onions, minced	2	
3	tbsp	soy sauce	50	mL
1	tbsp	white wine	15	mL
½	tsp	sugar	2	mL
1	tbsp	oil	15	mL

Garnish

2		green onions, finely chopped	2	

Have the fish cleaned and scaled but left whole with head and tail intact. Slash crosswise 3 times on both sides and sprinkle with salt.

Rinse and drain the black beans. Chop and mix with garlic, ginger, green onions, soy sauce, wine, sugar, and oil. Spread the mixture over the fish and place the fish on a heatproof platter.

Set up a pan for steaming. Place the platter on a rack, cover tightly, and steam for 15–20 minutes, or until the eye glazes. Remove from steamer. Sprinkle with green onions and serve on the same heatproof platter.

Lemon Chicken

A combination of flour and cornstarch adheres well to food and makes a crisper batter.

| | | chicken breasts, | |
| 3 | | boned and skinned | 3 |

Marinade

½	tsp	salt	2	mL
½	tbsp	white wine	10	mL
½	tbsp	soy sauce	10	mL
1	tbsp	cornstarch	15	mL
1	tbsp	cold water	15	mL
1		egg yolk	1	
⅛	tsp	pepper	Dash	

Final Seasoning Sauce

4	tbsp	sugar	50	mL
6	tbsp	fresh lemon juice *or*	75	mL
3	tbsp	lemon juice and	50	mL
3	tbsp	white rice vinegar	25	mL
6	tbsp	chicken stock	75	mL
½	tsp	salt	2	mL
3	tsp	cornstarch	15	mL
1	tsp	sesame oil	5	mL

Coating

6	tbsp	cornstarch	100	mL
3	tbsp	all-purpose flour	50	mL
		oil for deep frying		
		lemon slices		

Clean the chicken breasts and pat dry with paper towels. Mix the marinade ingredients in a large bowl and marinate the chicken breasts for about 30 minutes.

Mix the final seasoning sauce in a small bowl.

Combine the coating mixture.

Heat the oil for deep frying to 375 F (190 C), or until a small cube of bread tossed in browns quickly.

Remove chicken breasts from the marinade and dust with the coating mixture. Deep fry until a pale gold. Drain on paper towels and reserve.

Heat 1 tablespoon (15 mL) oil in the wok. Pour in the final seasoning sauce and stir until it comes to a boil. This sauce can be cooked ahead of time and reheated when needed.

At serving time, reheat the oil until very hot. Deep fry the chicken again until golden brown and heated through, about 1 minute. Drain and cut each breast into 5 or 6 slices. Arrange on a platter.

Pour the hot final seasoning sauce over the chicken slices. Garnish the platter with lemon slices.

Family Style Beef

1	lb	flank steak	500	g

Marinade

1	tsp	sugar	5	mL
2	tbsp	dark soy sauce	25	mL
2	tsp	cornstarch	10	mL
1	tbsp	cold water	15	mL
1	tbsp	oil	15	mL

1	lb	broccoli boiling water	500	g

Final Seasoning Sauce

1	tbsp	soy sauce	15	mL
2	tbsp	oyster sauce	25	mL
½	tbsp	white wine	10	mL
1½	tsp	sugar	7	mL
1	tsp	cornstarch	5	mL

	oil for deep frying	
8-10	very thin slices of ginger, peeled	8-10
2	green onions, sliced diagonally into ½-inch (1 cm) sections	2

Slice the beef against the grain as thinly as possible. Arrange in a bowl and add all the marinade ingredients except the oil. When the meat is coated with the mixture, add the oil. This prevents the slices from sticking together. Marinate at least 30 minutes or refrigerate in the marinade for the day.

Cut the broccoli into small flowerets. Add to the pot of boiling water and, when the water returns to a boil, remove the broccoli, drain, and plunge into cold water to stop the cooking and set the color. Drain thoroughly.

Mix the final seasoning sauce in a small bowl. Heat the oil for deep frying until it smokes. Remove beef slices from marinade and divide into 3 batches. Fry each batch for 30 seconds, using chopsticks for stirring. Remove each batch from oil and drain. (This step can be completed several hours before serving time.)

Heat 3 tablespoons (50 mL) of oil in a clean wok. Over high heat, add the ginger and green onions and let sizzle for a few seconds. Add the broccoli and stir fry until heated through. Add the beef and stir.

Pour in the final seasoning sauce. Mix well, stirring until the sauce has thickened and all ingredients are very hot. Place on a platter and serve.

Ginger Ice Cream

1 pint	vanilla ice cream	500 mL
3 pieces	stem ginger in syrup, finely chopped	3 pieces

Allow ice cream to soften slightly before adding the stem ginger. Return to freezer until needed.

On the day before: Prepare the ginger ice cream and store in freezer.

On the day: Prepare the marinade. Marinate the beef and chicken. Prepare the fish. Make the soup and reheat when needed. Mix final seasoning sauces.

Do first frying of beef and chicken. Cook final seasoning sauce for lemon chicken.

Steam the fish just before serving. A roasting pan with a rack makes a good steamer.

AN ITALIAN DINNER

Linguine with Fresh Tomato Sauce

Veal Chops with Vermouth

Braised Fennel or Leeks

Zabaglione

Recommended wines
Canteval Rouge
Chianti Classico (Brolio)
Chianti Classico Riserva Ducale (Ruffino)

to serve eight

The food of Italy is powerful, pungent, and exciting. It is also delicate, elegant, and aromatic.

Linguine with Fresh Tomato Sauce

If you can get or make fresh pasta, do so. If not a good dried noodle is fine. The sauce is quick to make.

6	tbsp	olive oil	75	mL
3	cloves	garlic, thinly sliced	3	cloves
6–8		ripe tomatoes, peeled, seeded, and coarsely chopped	6–8	
2	tbsp	fresh basil or	25	mL
2	tsp	dried	10	mL
3		anchovies, chopped (optional but good)	3	
1	tbsp	tomato paste	15	mL
		salt and pepper		
		grated Parmesan cheese		
1	lb	linguine	500	g

Heat the oil and add the garlic. Immediately add tomatoes. Sauté for 2–3 minutes, or until the tomatoes soften. Add basil, anchovies, tomato paste, and seasonings. Simmer for 2 minutes. Remove from heat and reserve.

Bring a large pot of water to a boil. Add the pasta and cook until tender. Drain well and mix with the sauce. Top each portion with Parmesan and serve extra cheese separately.

Veal Chops with Vermouth

6	veal chops, shoulder or rib	6
	salt and pepper	
	flour for dredging	
4 tbsp	butter	50 mL
½ cup	dry vermouth	125 mL
	juice and rind of 1 lemon	
½ cup	whipping cream	125 mL
	chopped parsley	

Season the chops with salt and pepper, then dredge in the flour. In a large frying pan, heat the butter until it sizzles. Add the chops and brown on both sides. Reduce heat to low and cover the pan. Simmer slowly, turning the chops occasionally. Cook until fork tender, about 30–45 minutes.

Remove the chops from the pan and keep warm.

Over high heat, add the vermouth and stir up any bits remaining at the bottom of the pan. Reduce the sauce by half. Add the lemon juice and rind and bring to a boil.

Add the cream and reduce the sauce again until slightly thickened. Add the parsley and pour the sauce over the chops.

Note: The dish can be left covered in a low oven for 30 minutes.

Variation: Top veal chops with tomato sauce and mozzarella cheese and run under the broiler before serving.

Braised Fennel or Leeks

Fennel has a licorice taste; Pernod will reinforce its flavor. If you use leeks omit the Pernod.

2	large	fennel bulbs, washed and trimmed of all outer leaves *or*	2	large
1	bunch	leeks split and washed	1	bunch
6	tbsp	butter	75	mL
½	cup	chicken stock	125	mL
		salt and pepper		
		generous pinch of ginger		
1	tbsp	Pernod or Sambuca	15	mL
½	cup	grated Parmesan cheese	125	mL

Preheat oven to 400 F (200 C).

Cut the fennel into 6 wedges.

Melt the butter in a baking dish and add the chicken stock. Arrange fennel on top. Spoon some stock over it and season with salt, pepper, and ginger.

Sprinkle with the Pernod and Parmesan. Cover and bake for 1 hour, or until tender. (The baking time for leeks is 45 minutes.)

Zabaglione

1	pint	fresh strawberries	500	mL
1½	cups	whipping cream	375	mL
3	tbsp	sugar	50	mL
8		egg yolks	8	
⅔	cup	Marsala or Amaretto	150	mL

Divide strawberries among 6 large wine glasses and refrigerate.

Whip the cream and, when almost thickened, add 1 tablespoon (15 mL) of the sugar and continue whipping until stiff. Refrigerate. In a heavy pot, combine egg yolks, remaining sugar, and the Marsala. Over medium heat, beat the mixture with a wire whisk until thick and creamy.

Place the pot over ice and cool, stirring occasionally. Fold in the whipped cream. Refrigerate the custard until needed.

To serve, spoon over berries.

On the day before: Make zabaglione and refrigerate.

On the day: Peel, seed, and chop the tomatoes. Flour chops. Prepare the fennel dish up to the baking stage. While chops are cooking, make the tomato sauce and cook the pasta.

A PICNIC BY THE RIVER FOR GOOD FRIENDS

Pork and Spinach Pâté

Chicken Legs with Apricot Sauce

Pasta Salad

Pickled Mushrooms

Lemon Tart

Recommended wines
Beaujolais Comte de Migieu (Poulet)
Inniskillin Maréchal Foch
Marquis de Cacères Rosé

to serve eight

Before summer theater or just as an escape from the hustle and bustle of the city, a picnic is a relaxing way to get together with friends.

Pork and Spinach Pâté

The pâté is lighter than most. The green spinach gives it a pretty look.

1	lb	fat pork	500 g
1	lb	spinach, cooked and well drained	500 g
½	tsp	grated nutmeg	2 mL
1		clove garlic, minced	1
½	tsp	ground allspice	2 mL
1	tsp	thyme	5 mL
1	tbsp	chopped parsley	15 mL
		salt and pepper	
2		hard-cooked eggs, chopped	2
8	oz	bacon to line mold	250 g

Preheat oven to 325 F (160 C).

Combine all ingredients except the bacon. Fry a small amount to taste for seasoning.

Line a bread pan or pâté mold with bacon, covering the bottom as well as the sides. Pack with the pork and spinach mixture. Cover the mold, place it in a pan of water to prevent the pâté from drying out, and bake for 1 hour. Cool and cover with foil. Over the foil, place a pan or other flat weight that just fits inside the top of the pâté. Weigh it down with three or four pounds of weight. Tin cans will do nicely. Chill the pâté, weighted down, for 24 hours before serving.

Chicken Legs with Apricot Sauce

This finger food, brown and crisp on the outside, tender and juicy within, is ideal for picnics. The apricot sauce gives it an out of the ordinary taste.

3	cups	chicken stock	750	mL
12		chicken drumsticks	12	
		flour for dredging		
		salt and pepper		
2		eggs	2	
2	tbsp	oil	25	mL
2	cups	bread crumbs	500	mL
2	tsp	marjoram	10	mL

Apricot Sauce

½	cup	white wine	125	mL
2		whole cloves	2	
1		stick cinammon	1	
6	oz	dried appricots	175	g
1½	cups	plain yogurt	375	mL
2	tbsp	finely chopped fresh mint	25	mL
		oil for deep frying		

Apricot Sauce

Bring wine, cloves, and cinnamon to a boil. Pour the sauce over the apricots. Soak for 24 hours. Remove cinamon stick. Purée the apricots in a blender or food processor together with some of the soaking liquid to make the mixture smooth. Fold in the yogurt. Add the chopped mint.

In a large saucepan, bring the chicken broth to a simmer. Add the chicken drumsticks and poach for 20 minutes. Let them cool in the broth, then remove and wipe dry. Combine flour, salt, and pepper in a small bowl. Beat the eggs with 2 tablespoons of oil in a second bowl. Combine bread crumbs, salt, pepper, and marjoram in a third bowl. Roll the drumsticks in the flour, dip them in the eggs, and coat with seasoned bread crumbs.

In a deep fryer or wok heat the oil to 350 F (180 C) or until a piece of bread fried in the oil turns brown immediately. Deep fry the legs in 2 or 3 batches until golden. Drain on a rack and cool. Serve with the apricot sauce.

Pasta Salad

A perfectly portable pasta.

1	lb	pasta shells	500 g
2	tbsp	olive oil	25 mL
		salt and pepper	
1		red onion, diced	1
1		red pepper, diced	1
1		green pepper, diced	1
1	lb	small shrimp or 3 4-oz (113 g) cans	500 g
1		8 oz (250 g) package frozen peas, defrosted	1

Lemon Vinaigrette

½	cup	olive oil	125 mL
3	tbsp	white wine vinegar	50 mL
3	tbsp	lemon juice	50 mL

6	green onions, white part only, finely chopped	6	
1	egg, beaten	1	
1 tbsp	chopped fresh basil	15	mL
	salt and pepper		

Boil the pasta shells in lots of boiling water until tender. Drain. Toss with olive oil. Season with salt and pepper. Combine with all the other salad ingredients.

Thoroughly combine all the vinaigrette ingredients, pour over the salad, and let marinate for at least 2 hours.

Pickled Mushrooms

These keep for 2–3 weeks.

| 1 | lemon, cut in half | 1 | |
| 1½ lb | small mushrooms | 750 | g |

Marinade

½ cup	white vinegar	50	mL
1	clove garlic, crushed	1	
1	medium onion, chopped	1	
1	bay leaf	1	
2 tbsp	tomato ketchup	25	mL
¾ cup	olive oil	175	mL
	salt and pepper		
4 tbsp	chopped parsley	50	mL

Bring a pot of water to a boil. Add the lemon and mushrooms. Let boil for 3 minutes. Discard the lemon. Remove the mushrooms and drain in a colander until you have made the marinade.

Combine the vinegar, garlic, onion, and bay leaf in a saucepan. Boil until the vinegar is reduced by half.

Off heat add the ketchup, then whisk in the oil.

Season well with salt and pepper. Add the mushrooms to the hot marinade. Toss to coat well. Marinate the mushrooms in the marinade for 24 hours, turning occasionally.

Taste for seasoning. Add parsley just before serving.

Lemon Tart

This filling resembles lemon curd. Its texture is thick and smooth although it contains neither flour nor cream.

Pastry

1½	cups	all-purpose flour	375	mL
3	tbsp	sugar	50	mL
8	tbsp	butter	125	mL
1		egg yolk	1	
2	tbsp	lemon juice	25	mL

Filling

3		eggs	3	
¾	cup	sugar or less	175	mL
9	tbsp	butter, melted	150	mL
2	tsp	grated lemon rind	10	mL
¾	cup	lemon juice	175	mL
		whipped cream (optional)		

Pastry

Preheat oven to 450 F (230 C).

Combine the flour and sugar. Cut in the butter and blend in the egg yolk and lemon juice.

Roll or pat out pastry ⅛-inch (3mm) thick. Place in 9-inch (23 cm) flan pan and trim excess. Prick and bake for 5 minutes.

Reduce oven temperature to 350 F (180 C).

Filling

Beat the eggs and sugar together. Add the melted butter and the lemon rind and juice. Pour into the pastry and bake for 20–25 minutes. Place under the broiler to brown the top.

Whipped cream may be spread on top of the lemon curd, if you wish.

Variation: This tart can also be made with oranges or limes.

On the day before: Make the pâté and refrigerate. Complete the chicken dish and refrigerate. Mix vinaigrette for pasta salad. Chop all the vegetables and refrigerate. Marinate the mushrooms.

On the day: Cook the pasta and dress it while still warm. Toss in the vegetables and the vinaigrette. Do not refrigerate.

Eggs Benedict — 74
Bouillabaisse
Coquilles St Jacques
Sole Fouquet — 116
Salmon Mousse
Sweet & Sour Pork 150
Le Coq au Vin [176]
Chicken Paprika
Lasagne 247
Enchiladas 248

Peach Amaretto Trifle

Maryland

Lemon squares:

Cake

Liqueurs & Coffee.

irish coffee

~~Spanish~~ Italian's - coffee.

P

quiche + salad —

Antipasto

3

Pate + cheese

Salad —

fresh fruit

Avacado dip

sole

orange chicken

3.27.
.87
4/7 4.

A ROMANTIC PICNIC

Lime Chicken

Mimosa Potato Salad

Hazelnut Sablées

Fresh Fruit and Cheese

Recommended wines
Liebfraumilch Rhinekeller
Moselmaid (Deinhard)
Wiltinger Scharzberg Zentral

to serve two

When you want to get away with the one you care about. . . .

Lime Chicken

A refreshing dish. Lime adds a fragrant taste to the chicken.

2	whole	chicken breasts, split	2
3	cups	chicken stock	750 mL

Marinade

¼	cup	lime juice	50 mL
1	clove	garlic, crushed	1
1	tbsp	dried tarragon	15 mL
2	tbsp	dried basil	10 mL
2	whole	green onions, finely chopped	2
½	cup	olive oil	125 mL
		salt and pepper	

Garnish

1	bunch	watercress, cleaned and trimmed	1 bunch
1	pint	strawberries, hulled	500 mL

Poach the chicken breasts in the stock for 15 minutes. Cool in the broth. Remove skin and bones. Cut chicken into slivers. Mix marinade ingredients in a food processor or blender. Pour over the chicken and marinate for 24 hours. Remove the chicken and garnish it with watercress and strawberries.

Mimosa Potato Salad

To make this salad taste even better, dress the potatoes while they are still hot when they absorb flavors more readily.

1	lb	potatoes, unpeeled	500	g
4	tbsp	distilled vinegar	50	mL
		salt and pepper		
2	tbsp	olive oil	25	mL
1		apple, peeled, cored, and thinly sliced	1	
2	tbsp	red wine vinegar	25	mL
½		Spanish onion, diced	125	mL
1	stalk	celery, finely chopped	1	
½	cup	mayonnaise	125	mL
1	tbsp	finely chopped parsley	15	mL
2		hard-cooked egg yolks, grated	2	
		spinach leaves		

Place potatoes in cold salted water. Add the distilled vinegar. Bring to a boil and cook until tender. Drain. Peel and slice while still warm. Season with salt and pepper and pour in the oil. Toss and leave to cool.

Soak the apple slices in the wine vinegar. Add to

cooled potatoes together with the onion and celery. Mix carefully. Add mayonnaise and parsley. Taste for seasoning. Sprinkle with the grated egg yolks.

Serve the potato salad on a bed of spinach leaves on a dinner plate.

Hazelnut Sablées

This recipe makes 30 cookies; too many for a picnic, but wonderful to have around anytime.

1	cup	unsalted butter	250 mL
1	cup	sugar	250 mL
1		egg yolk	1
1	tsp	vanilla extract	5 mL
2¼	cups	all-purpose flour	550 mL
1	cup	ground hazelnuts (filberts)	250 mL

Preheat oven to 350 F (180 C).
Grease 2 cookie sheets.

Cream the butter until light, and gradually add the sugar. Beat in the egg yolk and vanilla. Mix the flour with the ground nuts and beat into the creamed mixture very quickly. Shape into crescents. Bake 12–15 minutes, or until they are light brown. Cool on a rack. The sablées keep well—if they last.

Fresh Fruit and Cheese

Pears go well with brie. Some time before serving take the brie from the picnic basket and let it ripen in the sun.

On the day before: Prepare the whole menu in advance. Refrigerate the chicken and potato salad until needed for the picnic.

A BACKYARD BARBECUE

Grilled Shrimp

Butterflied Leg of Lamb

Potato Packages

Barbecued Leeks

Grilled Peppers

Raspberry Shortcake

Recommended wines
Côtes du Rhône Blanc (Mommessin)
Raimat Can Casal (Coniusa)
Lancorta (Landalan)
Hardy's Shiraz Cabernet

to serve eight

The art of barbecuing can be perfected by anyone without too much effort. Here is an excellent, easy to prepare menu which features lamb instead of the usual beef.

Grilled Shrimp

Messy but finger-licking good.

16		large shrimp, shells on	16	

Marinade

1	cup	olive oil	250	mL
3	tbsp	lemon juice	50	mL
2	tbsp	black peppercorns, crushed	25	mL
1	tsp	salt	5	mL
2	tsp	dried basil	10	mL

4 tbsp	finely chopped parsley	50	mL
2	medium-sized garlic cloves, finely chopped	2	
1 tsp	chili powder	5	mL

Split the shrimp down the back leaving tail attached and shell on. Combine marinade ingredients. Toss the shrimp in the marinade and refrigerate overnight. Grill the shrimp starting with shell side down, turning occasionally until pink. Serve with shell on.

Butterflied Leg of Lamb

You can buy boned lamb easily. Use a leg because the other cuts are too fatty for barbecuing and will cause flare-ups.

| 1 5–6 lb | leg of lamb, boned and butterflied | 3 | kg |

Marinade

1 cup	dry red wine	250	mL
¼ cup	lemon juice	50	mL
2 tbsp	apricot jam	25	mL
2 tbsp	tarragon vinegar	25	mL
2 tbsp	soy sauce	25	mL
1 clove	garlic, finely chopped	1	
2	onions, finely chopped	2	
1 tbsp	rosemary	15	mL
1 tbsp	marjoram	15	mL
1 large	bay leaf, crumbled	1	
1 tsp	salt	5	mL
1 tsp	ginger	5	mL
	pinch of ground cayenne pepper		

Remove any loose fat from the lamb.
Combine all marinade ingredients and simmer for

10 minutes, stirring occasionally. Brush the sauce over the lamb and marinate for 12 hours, turning several times.

Place meat on the grill, fat side up. Cook over medium coals for 40-50 minutes, basting frequently and turning the meat from time to time. Carve across the grain into thin slices. Because a lamb leg varies in thickness the cooking time should guarantee both well done and rare meat.

Potato Packages

To obtain a fluffier consistency make sure you use a baking potato for this recipe.

8	baking potatoes	8
2-3	onions, thinly sliced	2-3
	olive oil	
	salt and pepper	

Cut unpeeled potatoes into thin slices, accordion style, ⅔ of the way through the potato. Insert onion slices into the slits. Rub oil over the skins and sprinkle with salt and pepper. Wrap each potato in a double thickness of foil. Place on the grill and barbecue for about 1 hour, turning occasionally.

Barbecued Leeks

A different vegetable for the barbecue.

8	leeks	8
8 tbsp	butter	125 mL
	salt and pepper	

Split the leeks down to the root. Discard the coarse, dark green part. Wash well.

Place each leek on a piece of foil together with 1 tablespoon (15 mL) butter and the seasoning. Wrap tightly and barbecue for 15 minutes, turning twice. Remove foil and serve 1 leek per person.

Grilled Peppers

Use both red and green peppers, if available.

8	peppers	8

Place whole peppers on the grill. Barbecue, turning occasionally, until skin is black and peppers are soft. Remove from heat. Peel if desired. Slice and serve.

Raspberry Shortcake

This simple dessert is refreshing after a barbecue.

1½	lb	shortbread cookies	750 g
1	cup	chopped hazelnuts (filberts)	250 mL
8	tbsp	or more of juice drained from frozen raspberries	125 mL
		or	
8	tbsp	Framboise (raspberry liqueur)	125 mL
6	tbsp	sugar	100 mL
4	cups	unsweetened frozen raspberries, defrosted and drained	1 L

Garnish

10		whole hazelnuts (filberts)	
1	cup	whipping cream	250 mL

Raspberry Sauce (see below)

Process the cookies in a food processor or blender to make fine crumbs. There should be approximately 6 cups (1.5 L). Add the chopped hazelnuts. Reserve 2 cups (500 mL) of the mixture.

Slowly stir enough juice or liqueur into the remaining mixture to just bind it together without becoming pasty. Add more liquid if needed.

Sprinkle 1 tablespoon (15 mL) of sugar on the bottom of a 9 × 5 × 3-inch (23 × 13 × 8 cm) loaf pan. Pat a thin layer of the crumb mixture on the bottom, then up the sides. There will be some crumbs left over. Mix the remaining sugar with the well drained raspberries. Spoon half the fruit into the pan. Cover with the reserved crumbs; finish with the remaining raspberries. Sprinkle the leftover crumb mixture on top to cover. Pat down well.

Place a layer of foil on top, weighted down with 2 tin cans. See p. 133 re weighting a mold with tin cans. Refrigerate for 24 hours. Remove and run a small, sharp knife around the sides. Turn out onto a rectangular dish.

Whip the cream until it holds its shape and garnish the cake with 10 rosettes of whipped cream, each topped with a hazelnut.

To serve, remove the first slice then cut the portions with a knife dipped in hot water. Pour some raspberry sauce on each plate and place a raspberry shortcake slice on top.

Raspberry Sauce

> 2 15 oz   packages frozen rasp-
>   berries in sugar syrup

Purée raspberries in a food processor or blender. Sieve well to remove the seeds. Pour onto serving plates.

On the day before: Marinate the shrimp and refrigerate. Marinate the lamb and refrigerate. Prepare the raspberry shortcake and the sauce and refrigerate.

On the day: In the morning, prepare the leeks and potatoes. Wrap them in foil and refrigerate. Remove lamb and shrimp from the refrigerator 1 hour before needed. Unmold and decorate raspberry shortcake. Refrigerate until needed.

A CLASSIC COCKTAIL PARTY

Stuffed Lichees

Lucy's Chicken

Leek Tarts

Mushroom Rolls

Smoked Salmon Canapés

Lichees with Blue Cheese

Recommended wines
Andres Auberge
Codorniu Extra Sparkling
Frederic Chopin Sparkling (Wissembourg)
Villa Ambra (Fabiano)

to serve twenty

Making finger food for a cocktail party is time consuming and fiddly. Here are some simple hors d'oeuvres which don't take much time to prepare and are good to eat. They can be used for other occasions as well.

When you are planning the amounts to make, remember that one person can eat about six to eight small things.

Stuffed Lichees

Lichees are easy to fill because they have a natural cavity. If they are unavailable, spread the mixture on crackers or use as a stuffing for cherry tomatoes.

4	oz	cream cheese	125 g
2	oz	blue cheese	60 g
1	19-oz	can lichees, drained	540 g
20		or more almond	20
		slivers	

Beat together the 2 cheeses. With a pastry bag, pipe a little of the mixture into each lichee. Decorate with the almonds. Makes 20 pieces.

Lucy's Chicken

When I first made this chicken for a cocktail party, it was such a big hit it soon became known as Lucy's chicken. If the quantity is to be doubled or tripled and a bigger pan is used, the cooking liquid must be increased accordingly.

½ cup	dark soy sauce	125	mL
½ cup	light soy sauce	125	mL
½ cup	water	125	mL
½ cup	sugar	125	mL
3	star anise	3	
3	1-inch (2.5 cm) slices fresh ginger, smashed	3	
1 tsp	five spice powder	5	mL
5	chicken breasts, boned and skinned	5	

Garnish

1	carrot, julienned	1	
2	green onions, slivered	2	
1 inch	peeled ginger, slivered	2.5	cm

In a frying pan, bring to a boil the soy sauces, water, sugar, and seasonings. Reduce heat to simmer, slip in chicken breasts, and simmer 8 minutes on each side. Cool in the broth.

Remove the chicken and arrange on a platter in a wheel formation. Slice each breast on the diagonal into about 5 pieces. Scatter carrots, onions, and ginger on top. Makes about 30 pieces.

Leek Tarts

Simple to make and very rich and delicious. Mushrooms or zucchini can be substituted for the leeks.

Pastry

2	cups	all-purpose flour	500	mL
8	oz	cream cheese, cut in 8 chunks	250	g
8	oz	butter, cut in 8 chunks	250	mL

Filling

4	tbsp	butter	50	mL
3		leeks, washed and chopped	3	
1	cup	whipping cream	250	mL
		salt and pepper		

Pastry

Process the flour, cream cheese, and butter together in a food processor or with an electric mixer. Form pastry into a ball, then wrap and refrigerate for 30 minutes.

Filling

Melt the butter, add the leeks, and sauté until softened. Add the cream and cook until thickened. Season with salt and pepper.

Preheat oven to 425 F (220 C).

To assemble: Pat pastry into small muffin tins. Fill with leek mixture. Bake 15 minutes. These tarts can be reheated before serving. Makes about 30–36 tarts.

Mushroom Rolls

These are always popular, even with people who usually don't like curry.

15–20	pieces of bread, thinly sliced, crusts removed	15–20

8	tbsp	butter	125	mL
1	lb	mushrooms, finely chopped	500	g
1	tsp	curry powder	5	mL
2	tbs	lemon juice	25	mL
		salt and pepper		

Coating

| 1 | | egg, beaten | 1 | |
| | | dry bread crumbs | | |

Roll bread with a rolling pin as thin as possible. Butter each slice.

Melt remaining butter in a pan, add the mushrooms, and cook until all the moisture has disappeared. Add remaining ingredients and stir well. Cool.

Preheat oven to 425 F (220 C).

Spread about 1 tablespoon (15 mL) of the mushroom mixture on the buttered side of each slice of bread, roll up, and fasten with a toothpick. Dip the rolls in the beaten egg and coat with bread crumbs. Bake for 15 minutes on a greased cookie sheet and serve. Makes about 20 mushroom rolls.

Smoked Salmon Canapés

These canapé bases keep for several weeks in an airtight container.

Bases

| 1 | loaf | of bread, thinly sliced | 1 | |
| ½ | cup | butter, softened | 125 | mL |

Mousse

4	oz	cream cheese	125	g
½	cup	butter	125	mL
8	oz	smoked salmon	250	g
		pepper		
		fresh dill		

Preheat oven to 325 F (160 C).

Butter each bread slice. Using a small cookie cutter, cut into rounds. Bake for about 15–20 minutes, or until pale gold. Cool.

Purée cream cheese, butter, and smoked salmon in a blender or food processor until smooth. Season with pepper, if necessary. Spread mixture on bases and decorate each canapé with a piece of dill. Makes about 40 pieces.

On the day before: All dishes can be prepared ahead and refrigerated.

On the day: Let the chicken come to room temperature before serving. Reheat the leek tarts and the mushroom rolls on a rack over a cookie sheet (to heat evenly) in a 350 F (180 C) oven.

AFTER THEATER SUPPER

Fish Soup

Aïoli

Herb Bread

Chocolate Cake with Raspberry Sauce

Recommended wines
Cuvée les Amours (Hugel)
Mission Hill Chenin Blanc
Traminac (Navip)

to serve eight to ten

Prepare this menu ahead of time for friends return-
ing from the theater, or for any late evening occasion.

Fish Soup

You can also use clams, mussels, shrimp, or lobster
instead of fish.

4	tbsp	olive oil	50	mL
4		tomatoes, skinned and chopped, or	4	
2	tbsp	tomato paste	25	mL
1	cup	Spanish onion, chopped	250	mL
2		leeks, white part only, washed and chopped	2	
2		cloves garlic, crushed	2	
4	tbsp	chopped parsley	50	mL
2		bay leaves	2	
		pinch of saffron (optional)		

8 cups	boiling fish or chicken stock	2 L
2 lb	mixed filleted fish—grouper, halibut, monkfish, cod, snapper	1 kg

Heat the oil in a large pot. Add the vegetables and all the seasonings and sauté for about 4 minutes.

Add the boiling stock and cook on high heat for 10 minutes. Lower heat and add the fish. Simmer 10 minutes longer. If using shellfish simmer for only 7 minutes. Serve with aïoli.

Variation: This soup can be served puréed.

Aïoli

Aïoli is a pungent garlic mayonnaise that spikes the flavor of the fish soup. If your guests worry about the amount of garlic, give them a little parsley to chew—it's a natural breath freshener.

3 cloves	garlic, finely chopped	3 cloves
2	egg yolks	2
	juice of ½ lemon	
1-1½ cups	olive oil or vegetable oil	250-375 mL
¼ tsp	salt	1 mL
	freshly ground black pepper	

Place garlic and egg yolks in a blender or food processor. Process. With the machine running, add half the lemon juice, then slowly drizzle the oil into the mixture until it is all absorbed. Add the remaining lemon juice, salt, and pepper to taste. If the mixture is too thick add 1-2 tablespoons (15-25 mL) hot water to thin it out.

Herb Bread

1		long loaf of French bread	1	
8	oz	butter	250	mL
2		anchovy fillets, finely chopped	2	
2	tsp	tarragon	10	mL
2	tsp	thyme	10	mL
2	tbsp	chopped fresh chives	25	mL
4	tbsp	chopped parsley	50	mL
		juice of ½ lemon		
		pepper		

Beat together the butter, anchovies, herbs, lemon juice, and pepper. Cut the bread into thin slices. Spread each slice with the herb butter. Reassemble as a loaf and wrap in foil.

Preheat oven to 425 F (220 C).

Place the bread on a cookie sheet and bake for 10 minutes. Remove foil and bake for another 5 minutes, or until the bread has browned.

Chocolate Cake with Raspberry Sauce

This incredible cake resembles a chocolate bar; therefore, use an eating chocolate rather than a baking chocolate.

1	lb	European bittersweet chocolate	500	g
10	tbsp	butter	150	mL
4		eggs	4	
2	tbsp	sugar	25	mL
1	tbsp	all-purpose flour	15	mL

Garnish

1	cup	whipping cream	250	mL

Raspberry Sauce (see right)

Preheat oven to 400 F (200 C).

Butter a deep 8-inch(20.5 cm) cake pan or charlotte mold. Line the bottom with parchment paper.

In a heavy pot, melt the chocolate and butter over low heat, stirring occasionally. Cool.

Beat together the eggs and sugar with an electric beater until the mixture triples in volume and is very thick and mousselike. Quickly fold in the flour. Mix a quarter of the mixture into the melted chocolate, then fold the chocolate into the remaining egg mixture.

Pour the batter into the cake pan. Bang it on the counter to remove any air bubbles. Bake for 15 minutes.

The cake will still be runny in the center when removed from the oven. Cool, then freeze overnight. Whip the cream until it stands in soft peaks. Turn the cake out onto a platter and decorate with the whipped cream. Serve each slice with a raspberry sauce.

Raspberry Sauce

| 2 | 15 oz | packages frozen raspberries in sugar syrup. | 2 | (425 g) |

Purée the raspberries in a food processor or blender. Sieve well to remove the seeds and chill.

On the day before: Everything can be prepared ahead of time. The chocolate cake will keep in the freezer for a month. The aïoli will keep a week, stored in the refrigerator.

On the day: Decorate the cake. Pop herb bread into the oven while the soup is reheating.

GOURMET ON THE GO

The following two menus are designed for people on the go. Each menu takes an hour to prepare, perfect for working people and busy homemakers who have a desire for good food but little time to spend in the kitchen.

MENU ONE

Onion Soup with Tomato Pesto

Chicken Breast with Poire William

Linguine

Boston Lettuce with Leek Vinaigrette

Mango Fool

Recommended wines
Rock Blanc
Paarl Riesling
Château des Charmes Primeur Rouge

to serve two

Onion Soup with Tomato Pesto

A beautiful porcelain color, highlighted with red swirls.

2 cups	chicken stock	500	mL
1	small potato, peeled and diced (about ½ cup)	125	mL
1 cup	Spanish onion, sliced	250	mL
1	small clove garlic, minced	1	
¼ cup	whipping cream salt and pepper	50	mL

Put stock, potato, onion, and garlic in a pot. Simmer until potato is tender. Purée in a blender or food processor until smooth. Add the cream, season with salt and pepper and reheat. Pour into soup bowls and serve with the tomato pesto swirled on top.

Tomato Pesto

1	large tomato, seeded and chopped	1
1 tsp	tomato paste	5 mL
1 tsp	dried basil or	5 mL
1 tbsp	chopped fresh basil	15 mL
1 tsp	tarragon	5 mL
1 tbsp	grated Parmesan cheese	15 mL
	salt and pepper	

Place all the ingredients in a blender or food processor and purée until smooth.

Chicken Breasts with Poire William

Can be made with apples, or with peaches in the summer. Change the liqueur to correspond with the fruit.

6 tbsp	unsalted butter	100 mL
2	pears or other fruit, peeled and sliced in eighths	2
1	large whole chicken breast, split, boned, and skinned	1
	salt and pepper	
½ cup	dry white wine	50 mL
½ cup	whipping cream	125 mL
2 tbsp	Poire William or other fruit brandy	25 mL

In a frying pan heat half the butter until it sizzles. Sauté the pears until barely tender and slightly browned. Remove and keep warm. Add the remaining butter to the pan. Season the chicken with salt and pepper. Place in the pan and cook on medium heat for 2–3 minutes, depending on the thickness of the meat. Turn and cook the other side for another 2 minutes. Pour in the wine and let boil until it evaporates, then add the cream and Poire William. Reduce until cream thickens slightly. Scatter in reserved pears. Serve with linguine.

Linguine

8	oz	fresh linguine	250	g
4	tbsp	butter, softened	50	mL
		salt and pepper		

Bring a pot of water to a boil. Boil the linguine for 1–3 minutes, depending on the thickness. Drain well, coat with butter, and season with salt and pepper.

Boston Lettuce with Leek Vinaigrette

Dressing

9	tbsp	olive oil	125	mL
3	tbsp	white wine vinegar	50	mL
1		small leek, white part only, washed and finely chopped	1	
		salt and pepper		
1		small head Boston lettuce	1	
		green part of leek, washed and julienned		

Combine first 3 ingredients in a jar and shake well. Season to taste. Arrange the lettuce leaves on a salad plate. Scatter with julienned leeks and pour over enough dressing to moisten the lettuce.

Mango Fool

Use papaya or strawberries for a flavor change.

2	mangoes, peeled and pitted	2
¼ cup	sugar, or to taste	50 mL
1 cup	whipping cream	250 mL

Reserve half a mango and slice it for garnish. Combine remaining mango and sugar in a food processor or blender. Purée. Taste for sweetness and add more sugar if necessary. Whip the cream until it holds its shape. Fold in the mango purée. Chill well. Serve in pretty glass dishes, garnished with slices of reserved mango.

MENU TWO

Mushrooms in Cream Sauce

Flank Steak with Wine Sauce

Low Calorie French Fries

Grated Zucchini

Brie Fondue

Recommended wines
Moreau Rouge
Paul Masson Cabernet Sauvignon
Rubesco (Lungarotti)

to serve two

Mushrooms in Cream Sauce

2	slices French bread, 1-inch thick (2.5 cm)	2
1 clove	garlic, split	1 clove
	olive oil	

8 oz	mushrooms, sliced	250 g
2 tbsp	butter	25 mL
1 clove	garlic, minced	1 clove
2 tbsp	fresh dill, finely chopped	25 mL
½ cup	whipping cream salt and pepper	125 mL

Preheat oven to 350 F (180 C).

Rub the bread with the cut garlic clove and brush with a little olive oil. Bake the bread for 10-15 minutes, or until golden brown.

On high heat, melt the butter until sizzling. Add the mushrooms and minced garlic. Sauté for 1-2 minutes, or until mushrooms become limp. Add the dill and cream and reduce until the sauce thickens. Season well.

Pile on top of toasted bread. Serve at once.

Flank Steak with Wine Sauce

Flank steak has at least two practical advantages—it has little fat and it is inexpensive. But it must be carved in thin diagonal slices across the grain or the meat will be tough.

Marinade

2 tbsp	Dijon mustard	25 mL
1	clove garlic, crushed	1
1 tbsp	lemon juice	15 mL
1 tbsp	soy sauce	15 mL
¼ cup	olive oil or vegetable oil	50 mL
1 lb	flank steak	500 g
1 tsp	thyme	5 mL

Wine Sauce

| ¼ cup | dry red wine | 50 mL |
| ¾ cup | beef broth | 175 mL |

1	small clove garlic, crushed	1
2 tsp	Dijon mustard	10 mL
3 tbsp	butter	50 mL

Marinade

Mix the mustard, garlic, lemon juice, and soy sauce. Whisk in the olive oil.

Score the steak in a diagonal grid pattern, rub in the thyme, and spread with the marinade. Marinate at least 1 hour. If possible marinate longer; several hours in the marinade will tenderize the meat further and allow flavors to deepen. Preheat broiler. Broil the steak about 3 minutes on each side for rare. Carve against the grain into thin, diagonal slices and serve with wine sauce.

Wine Sauce

In a small saucepan, boil the wine on high heat until it is reduced by half. Add the broth, garlic, and mustard and reduce the mixture a little more. On low heat, swirl in the butter until it is absorbed.

Low Calorie French Fries

2	baking potatoes	2
2 tbsp	olive oil or vegetable oil	25 mL
	salt and pepper	

Preheat oven to 400 F (200 C). Peel the potatoes and cut as for thick french fries. Lay potatoes on an oiled baking sheet and brush them with olive oil. Season with salt and pepper. Bake for 30 minutes.

Grated Zucchini

Simple and quick.

| 2 | zucchini | 2 |
| | salt | |

3 tbsp	butter	50 mL
	pepper	

Grate the zucchini. Sprinkle with salt and leave 15 minutes. Squeeze dry. Heat the butter until sizzling. Add the zucchini and stir fry about 1 minute. Season with pepper.

Brie Fondue

Brie melts well and the brown sugar enhances the mellow taste.

4 oz	brie	125 g
1 tbsp	or more brown sugar	15 mL
1 tbsp	sliced almonds or walnuts	15 mL
	fresh strawberries	
	crackers	

Preheat oven to 375 F (190 C).

Cut the brie into pieces and remove the rind. Pack in a small ovenproof dish. Sprinkle with brown sugar and almonds. Bake 8-10 minutes, or until the brie melts. Serve with strawberries and crackers to dip into the hot, melted cheese.

WINE
PARTIES
AND OTHER
GOOD
THINGS

*From wine what
sudden friendships spring*

—JOHN GAY

WINE TASTING PARTY

One of the most pleasurable methods of enlarging your knowledge of wine is to give a wine tasting party. Such an enterprise can range from a small "bring your own" get-together with a few close friends to a large, gala event.

Whatever the size of your party, there are certain rules to follow.

Choosing the Wines

Get help from liquor board wine consultants, vintners, importers, and anyone you know who drinks wine.

Offer a variety of wines including several which are similar, e.g., inexpensive dry reds and a selection of German-style wines from different countries.

Count on 12 servings per 750 mL bottle. This allows enough wine for each guest to appreciate the bouquet and the taste.

Preparation

Have on hand a sufficient number of all-purpose wine glasses. These can be rented inexpensively or obtained free of charge from most companies that provide the wine for tasting.

If you're serious about your wine tasting, cover all the bottles so that your palate will not be influenced by names, prices, or labels.

Bring all red wines to room temperature. Refrigerate the whites, rosés, and sparkling wines for about two hours before serving.

Provide a basin of water for rinsing glasses between tastings and a bowl for dumping the remains.

Food

Some kind of simple food is necessary to clear the palate between tastings. French bread and cream crackers do this best. Avoid salted crackers and sharp cheese.

Tasting Tips

Pour one or two ounces (30 to 60 g) of wine into a glass.

Hold it up to the light. Note color, check for clarity. In red wines purple suggests youth; pale brownish-red is an indication of age.

Check the bouquet. Swirl the wine around the glass so that it coats the sides. Lift to your nose and inhale. Take your time.

Taste. Don't sip or gulp. Take a generous amount into your mouth; let it move through your teeth, over and under your tongue, rolling it around to get the "feel" of it.

Swallow. Stop and think. How does it taste? Is there an aftertaste? What's your verdict?

The smell of cigarette smoke and the taste of wine are not compatible. Try to restrict smoking to other rooms.

Provide pencil and paper. Guests might like to make notes.

Your guests might even like to rate the wines. (See tasting guide on page 23.)

COLD WINE DRINKS AND PUNCHES

The following are recipes for a few mixed wine drinks which help to extend your wine dollar.

Bucks Fizz or Mimosa

1	bottle sparkling white wine or champagne orange juice	750 mL

In each champagne flute or wine glass, mix equal quantities or orange juice and white wine or champagne.

16 servings

Kir

| 1 | bottle white wine | 750 mL |
| | Cassis | |

In each wine glass, mix 1 teaspoon (5 mL) cassis with 4 ounces (125 mL) wine.

8 servings

Frambrosia

| 1 | bottle sparkling white wine or champagne Framboise raspberries | 750 mL |

In each champagne flute or wine glass, pour ½ ounce (15 mL) Framboise. Add white wine or champagne. Float a raspberry on top.

8 servings

Black Velvet

| 1 | bottle sparkling white wine | 750 mL |
| 2 | bottles stout | |

In each wine glass, mix equal quantities of wine and stout.

16 servings

Spritzer

1	bottle white wine	750 mL
	soda water	
	lemon or lime slices	

Traditionally this drink consists of one-half wine and one-half soda. However, most people prefer two-thirds wine and one-third soda. Top each glass with a lemon or lime slice.

12–16 servings

Northern Mist

1	bottle sparkling white wine	750 mL
1	10-oz (283 g) package frozen strawberries, without sugar	1
2	bottles ginger ale	750 mL each

Mix wine and ginger ale in a punch bowl. Float frozen unthawed strawberries on top.

16 servings

Sangria

1	bottle full-bodied red wine	750 mL
1 oz	cognac or brandy juice of 2 oranges juice of 1 lemon	30 mL
½ cup	sugar, or to taste sliced fresh fruit	125 mL

Mix all ingredients except sliced fruit in a pitcher and chill. Add fruit (apple slices, orange wedges, or any other fresh fruit). To serve, pour into large tumblers.

12 servings

HOT WINE PUNCHES

Originally, wassail, meaning "in good health," was used to propose a toast to an honored guest. The guest would reply, "Drink hail!" Later, in "merrie olde England," the health of Christmas revelers was toasted with spiced wine or sherry and wassail became the traditional Christmas Eve drink. Glögg is the Swedish version of wassail.

Mulled wine is another popular cold weather drink which originated in England where homes were poorly heated and people were looking for something to warm their insides.

To make mulled wine in the old days, a poker was heated on an open fire and then plunged into the glass.

Here are recipes for some of these traditional hot punches:

Wine Wassail

1	bottle slightly sweet red wine	750	mL
¼ tsp	coriander seeds	1	mL
2	whole cloves cinnamon sticks lemon rind, grated	2	

Bring wine, coriander, and cloves to a boil. Pour into tumblers, add cinnamon sticks, and garnish with slivers of lemon rind.

8 servings

Glögg

1	bottle dry red wine	750	mL
½ cup	sugar	125	mL
5-7	cardamom seeds, slipped from pod	5-7	
4	whole cloves	4	
1	cinnamon stick	1	
1	strip orange rind	1	
½ cup	raisins	125	mL
½ cup	blanched almonds	125	mL

Add the wine, sugar and spices to a pan and heat. Pour into cups. Garnish with raisins and almonds.

8 servings

Mulled Wine

1 cup	sugar	250 mL
3 cups	boiling water	750 mL
	rind and juice of 1 lemon	
18	whole cloves	18
1	cinnamon stick	1
2	bottles dry red wine	750 mL each
	grated nutmeg	

Dissolve sugar in boiling water. Add the lemon rind, lemon juice, cloves, and cinnamon stick. Boil for 15 minutes, or until syrupy. Strain into a double boiler and add the wine. Heat until piping hot but do not boil. Serve flecked with grated nutmeg. *14 servings*

WHAT TO DO WITH LEFTOVER WINE

When wine is left over from a party (or if, after opening a bottle you decide you don't like it), here are a few ideas to prevent waste.

Figs in Red Wine

Figs can be preserved in wine for months. Put into attractive jars, they make great Christmas gifts.

3 cups	dry red wine	750 mL
2	unpeeled lemons, sliced	2
2	unpeeled oranges, sliced	2
2	cinnamon sticks	2
4	whole cloves	4
1 cup	water	250 mL
1 lb	dried figs	500 g

Place all the ingredients except the figs in a saucepan and bring to a boil. Add the figs and simmer for 2 minutes.

Let cool and refrigerate the figs in the wine mixture for 1 week. Pack in jars, cover with the wine, and seal with lids.   *Yields 3-8 oz (250 mL) jars.*

Prunes in White Wine

1 lb	pitted prunes	500 g
2 cups	sugar	500 mL
1 cup	water	250 mL
1 cup	dry white wine	250 mL

Combine the sugar and water and boil for 10 minutes, or until a syrup forms. A candy thermometer should register 220°F.(110°C.). Add the wine. Let cool and refrigerate the prunes in the wine mixture for 1 week. Store in jars.   *Yields 3-8 oz (250 mL) jars.*

Wine Vinegar

Transfer ends of wine bottles to two crocks, one for white and one for red wine. When you have accumulated a sufficiently large quantity, add about 4 tablespoons (50 mL) of red wine vinegar to the crock of red wine and 4 tablespoons (50 mL) white wine vinegar to the crock of white wine. Cover and let sit 1 month before using. This wine vinegar can serve as a starter for subsequent crocks.

CHEESE

"Cheese makes wine sing": an old French proverb. Cheese is the perfect partner for wine as the two tastes complement and contrast each other.

Canadian cheese consumption is increasing and thanks to effective refrigeration and available imports, better food shops in major Canadian cities are able to stock a remarkable selection of cheeses.

Cheese making in Canada is a comparatively young

industry. Cheese factories were not established until the second half of the last century. The early British settlers made Cheddar on their farms and other immigrants tried to imitate the cheeses of their native homelands. As a result we now have a wide range of excellent Canadian-made cheeses.

The more popular cheeses available today can be divided into five basic categories:

1. Hard Cheeses
They include the various Cheddars and their English cousins. The best known of the English cousins is Cheshire, which is a truly British cheese available in red, white, and blue colors. Other examples of the English hard cheeses are Double Gloucester, Lancashire, Leicestershire, Wensleydale, Windsor Red, Sage Derby (made from herbs and Cheddar), and the Welsh favorite Caerphilly (made with buttermilk). The Irish Wexford is also a hard cheese.

Parmesan is another hard cheese now manufactured in Canada. Concurrent with the popularity of Italian food, its demand has increased in recent years. Parmesan is often sold in grated form; however, it is best when *freshly* grated. Parmigiano-Reggiano is the best imported Parmesan. Matured for two to three years, it is shaped in wheels. Parmesan is rated by its year just like wine. The older the cheese, the better it is.

Other hard cheeses are the Swiss Emmenthal and Gruyère, both distinguishable by the holes which are left in during processing. From Scandinavia comes the Jarlsberg, known as a "baby" Emmenthal because of its slightly milder flavor.

2. Semisoft Cheese
The semisofts include the white and soft-textured Havarti and mozzarella. Because mozzarella melts so well, it is particularly popular for use in pizzas and other Italian foods. A Canadian mozzarella is now available.

In the semisoft category as well are the unripened or

fresh types, such as cottage cheese, cream cheese, and ricotta.

Munster (or Muenster) is also a semisoft cheese. Encased in a brick-red skin, it has a distinctive aroma, just like the original made in the French Alsace.

Oka is the famous cheese of Quebec, originally made by the Trappist Monks in the town of Oka near Montreal. The recipe is based on a Port Salut formula and the cheese has a very mild aroma and piquant flavor. The Monks sold their recipe to a wine company which then sold it to another firm that is still making it today.

3. Surface Mold Ripened

The soft cheeses that ripen naturally in a matter of days include Brie and Camembert. Canada now makes its own unstabilized Brie which compares well with imported varieties. It is certainly highly recommended by tyrophiles (cheese lovers) who, incidentally, report that the great-grandson of the famous French painter, Pierre Auguste Renoir, is making Brie in the province of Alberta.

Another cheese in this category is St. Andre, a very rich cheese made with triple cream.

4. The Blues

The veined types known as blue cheese include Roquefort, Gorgonzola and Stilton. Stilton, with its wrinkled, dull crust differs from the other two in texture and appearance and is a strong claimant for the title "King of Cheese." By the same token, Italians claim that their Gorgonzola, made in the town of Gorgonzola near Milan, is "Il Re de Formaggio."

Roquefort is made in southwestern France, and every year gastronomes make a pilgramage to the caves near the town of Roquefort where the cheese is made. It is aged for three to six months and then stamped with a red emblem depicting a sheep. (By international agreement this mark cannot be used by any other blue cheese manufacturer.)

Danish Blue is another popular blue cheese.

In Canada we have our own creamy blue cheese known as Ermite. It is made by the Benedictine monks in the basement of the Abbey of St. Benoit du Lac in Southern Quebec.

5. Skim Milk Cheese

Despite the great interest in these cheeses by the calorie-conscious, there is some confusion about them. Even cheeses made from skim milk can be high in fat because cream has been added to the curds. The deciding factor is how much fat the final product contains.

Low fat cheeses contain from 0 to 15% fat; among them cottage cheese is the most common fresh type. Examples of low fat ripened cheese are skim milk Cheddar, Ricotone, and St. Otho.

Don't be fooled! No low fat cheese tastes as good or has the same creamy texture as high and full fat cheese.

BIBLIOGRAPHY

Anderson, Burton. *Vino,* Little, Brown and Company, 1980.

Johnson, Hugh. *Pocket Encyclopedia of Wine,* Mitchell Beazley Publishers Limited, 1981.

Johnson, Hugh. *The World Atlas of Wine,* Mitchell Beazley Publishers Limited, 1978.

Lichine, Alexis. *Alexis Lichine's Encyclopedia of Wines and Spirits,* Alfred A. Knopf, Inc., 1981.

Olken, Charles; Singer, Earl; and Roby, Norman. *The Connoisseurs' Handbook of California Wines.* Alfred A. Knopf, Inc., New York, 1980.

Saintsbury, George. *Notes on a Cellar-Book,* Macmillan London Ltd., 1978.

Vandyke Price, Pamela. *The Taste of Wine,* Random House, Inc., New York, 1975.

INDEX